BATS, PADS AND GLADIATORS
A Miscellany of Gloucestershire Cricket

*'Gloucestershire is the greatest county of all because
we've had the greatest cricketers – WG and WR. I mean,
you couldn't get two better cricketers than that.'*

Bryan 'Bomber' Wells.

CHARLES WOOD

Illustrated by the author

HALSGROVE

To Chris and Gareth

First published in Great Britain in 2012

Also by Charles Wood:
How to Survive in Somerset
Surviving Another Somerset Year
Exmoor Amour
Bats, Pads and Cider – A Miscellany of Somerset Cricket

Publisher's Disclaimer
As is well known, Halsgrove have disowned Mr Wood on many occasions
in the past and this particular volume is no exception. The views expressed herein arise
entirely from the fevered brain of Mr Wood who remains
entirely responsible for them, the Publisher is pleased to say.

British Library Cataloguing-in-Publication Data
A CIP record for this title is available from the British Library

ISBN 978 0 85704 169 2

HALSGROVE
Halsgrove House,
Ryelands Business Park,
Bagley Road, Wellington, Somerset TA21 9PZ
Tel: 01823 653777   Fax: 01823 216796
email: sales@halsgrove.com

Part of the Halsgrove group of companies
Information on all Halsgrove titles is available at: www.halsgrove.com

Printed and bound in China by Everbest Printing Co Ltd

The Naming of Parts

Acknowledgements

I am indebted to Julian, an important decision maker at my publishers, who had mused that a book on Gloucestershire cricket of 'then and now' wouldn't go amiss - a bit like having an MOT at the doctor's.

I agreed in principIe, referred to the price of diesel and to an archive of match footage and interviews that I'd filmed during the 1990s now sat in the middle of a draughty warehouse at the TSW TV Archive in Plymouth. Given the County's recent fortunes, a fillip of nostalgia was a sound idea even if it might be a knee-jerk response that over time would become as forgotten as video tape.

Anyway, my grateful thanks must go to David Graveney, David Allen, Graham Wiltshire, Jack Russell, and Andy Stovold for having taken the time to chat in odd places. Warm thanks must also extend to to the late Bryan 'Bomber' Wells and Bert Avery for their memories, and to the late Peter West for the hospitable after-noons of cricket talk in Duntisbourne Abbots.

Special gratitude, moreover, to Goose for keeping me up to date with cricketing trifles, to Gareth and Chris for providing me a sunny terrace on which to write, to Samuel the Sage of Nevis, to Martin the Bat Maker, and also to my loving wife who, having come to avidly learn the rudimentary rules of cricket, has held me steadfast to the task through her tireless encouragement.

My thanks to boot to my cat for sharing the excitements and excrutiations of cricket radio commentaries that have, inevitably, caused key-pad tapping delays. And, as a consequence, I additionally thank my publishing editor Steven Pugsley for his patience, and regret the need for his frequent nudges.

Most importantly of all, I thank Gloucestershire County Cricket Club, lovers of the Shire, and the 'cricket family', who together make the long days of warm sunshine so special for match day scribblings in a 'Moleskine'.

Wiveliscombe,
Summer 2012

A Preface of Clustered Dreams

'Though cricket is changing
And few are the traces
Remaining of W.G.
(Why the ball smaller?
Why the stumps taller?
Why twenty minutes for tea?)
Gloucestershire still is
"The home of the Graces"
To every old buffer like me.'

E.V.L.

Sometimes it's nice to lose oneself in a cricket crowd where Gloucestershire is known simply as the 'Shire'.

'Whatcha, Zumbeamer!' said Goose, loudly. 'Why bovver lookin' up at Royals and Bears when you can look down at Zum, eh?'

I wasn't sure whether Goose was giving me a neighbourly Shire geography lesson about Worcestershire, Warwickshire and Somerset or reminding me of Shire etiquette. What I did know was that he was drawing attention to me.

'Shush,' I said in a stage whisper, 'I'm incognito.' Certainly I was trying to be, but perhaps less so than a batter in a grilled helmet. To tell the truth, when it came to showing loyalty, Goose never hid under a bushel.

'Hey, you Zumbeamer?' growled a heavy bloke in earshot wearing a Walton Cricket Club sweatshirt. I did a quick calculation. He either came from the Taunton side of Glastonbury or from Wetherby in the heart of Yorkshire, and was lost. Given his accent I reckoned on the former, and that made him quite local.

Look down at Zum, hey? Oh, thanks a lot Goose, I thought.

So, before I committed myself to revealing my alter ego, I wracked my brains to remember if I'd written anything memorable that could possibly be construed as incriminating. I needn't have bothered. Goose answered on my behalf. 'Yep. He is.'

Given the size of 'Mister Walton', I remained a little hesitant in confirming Goose's assertion. 'Er, maybe.'

'Yes, you are. I know you are. We're following you.' The joys of Twitter and blogging put a whole different slant to the connotations of our brave New World.

I suppose Goose was purely trying to be helpful. I had broken it gently that, aided by a scribbled Moleskine full of anecdotes and observations, I'd volunteered to write about Shire cricket and family ties had already got me whooshing back and forth along the M5.

His sudden facial freeze had broken into an expression of alarm at the news. And he became forthcoming in his directness. 'For Gawd's sake, write something cheerful. Don't go waffling on about catastrophes. Remember, you're a country mouse at heart, so stay in your comfort zone.'

Happily, for me, cricket was originally a farm thing. Labourers became the first professionals, often earning a quarter of their annual earnings from playing in a single afternoon's cricket match. And although the purse strings may be tight and knotted these days, the Shire's rural nature, like its form on the pitch, has remained fairly constant.

Admittedly, things were better at the very beginning. It's accepted the county finally got its act together to form itself into a first-class cricket county in 1870. And although not quite the same at all as winning the County Championship, on four glorious occasions during the ensuing decade the Shire delighted in being declared 'Champion County'.

Around the same time, the Unification of Italy and Germany had been encouraged by nationalistic dreams. And in the same way Italy had Cavour and Germany had Bismarck grasping the reins of development, the Shire had a strongminded family of Graces doing the same. Inspiring by example, they heightened the bar of cricketing excellence. Out of a keen cluster of little clubs like Apney Crucis, and Lydney, Thornbury and Moreton-in-Marsh, there arose the grass roots talent to sustain future ambition.

Yet, since those successes of long ago, winning the County Championship proper remains a chimera. Yes, there has been many a good year in the county of W. G. Grace, G.L. Jessop, and R.C. 'Jack' Russell MBE, but there have also been more than a fair share of tears and doldrums both at Bristol and Gloucester, not to mention Cheltenham.

Enter a new chapter. Resplendent in blue pyjamas the county pros now call themselves 'Gladiators'. Hope springs eternal, and cricketing tales are legion. Take as examples the cricketing 'spirit' upon Sheepscombe's Laurie Lee Field, or those Pratt Cup cricketers changing into whites in the billiard room of a North Nibley mansion overshadowed by Breakheart Hill.

Neither should one overlook the parrot that squawked 'GLAWSTER!' nor the bizarre connections embedded as far afield as the islands of Nevis and Corfu. What one soon realizes is that here is a cricketing county with a wide following, full to the brim with eccentricity and odd statistics. Randomly for instance, 9, 1, 2, 1, 3, 1, wasn't a mobile number, but Bill Athey's first six innings for England, and the top scorer in each Northants innings at Bristol in 1998 was 'extras'.

Admittedly, the mantra, these days, is 'slowly, slowly'. The current Championship objective is just to get out of Division 2, and in vogue one-day celebrations come as fleeting lights.

Lest we forget, Shire life is not all about being Number One. The county's richness of character and anecdote drawn from over the years, and alluded to within these pages, will, I hope, act as balm on any burning desires that niggle.

The Founding of Gloucestershire County Club

W.G. Grace's dad, Dr Henry Mills Grace was the chap responsible for the early days of Gloucestershire County Cricket Club when he founded Mangotsfield Cricket Club. Later this amalgamated with Coalpit Heath Cricket Club to become West Gloucestershire Cricket Club.

Henry eventually achieved his healthy ambition in early June 1870 when Gloucestershire County Cricket Club played their first county match. This was against Surrey on the flat grass swathes of Bristol's Durdham Downs. W.G. captained, and led the Shire to a 51 run victory.

The first game at Nevil Road was on 1st July 1889. The visitors then were Lancashire. And in the same year the Shire established their Club's colours of Fawn, Brown, Pale Grey, Dark Green, Red and Navy Blue.

'Curiosities of Cricket'
Cricket Fatalities From the Earliest Records Until 1897
by An 'Old Cricketer'

'One death from falling on a stump, two from heart disease, two from over exertion, one from snake bite, another by being crushed between railway trucks while recovering the ball, and one from falling over a cliff whilst following the ball.'

A Trying Top Order

ONE

Cat-Flap and Parrot

So do I breathe the hayblown airs of home,
And watch the sea-green elms drip birds and shadows,
And as the twilight nets the plunging sun
My heart's keel slides to rest among the meadows.

Laurie Lee, *Home From Abroad.*

It was the beginning of the 1997 cricket season. As we strolled among the primroses of his Cotswold garden I asked Peter West, the retired BBC cricket
commentator, a question. The Kentish boy had become a sage of Gloucestershire, caught up in the county's romance from Duntisbourne Abbotts.

Having pondered for a short while, Peter responded. 'Hopes for the future? Well,
we must all have those. It's time Gloucestershire won the Championship. I don't
think it's going to happen tomorrow, as it were. But it seems to me that the spirit
in the county is jolly good. I think the structure is right, we've got some promising young players coming, and who knows, it's a funny old game.'

Funny old game? Absolutely, I thought. However, Peter didn't seem quite his
usual wry humoured self. I mean, this was the man who had described himself
as a 'flannelled fool and muddied oaf'. Something other than Shire cricket was
obviously troubling him.

Eventually, he broke the news to me with a 'Did you know … ?'

The Son of Slad and soul of the Shire, Laurie Lee the inspirational novelist and
poet, had passed on. I kept a stiff upper lip at the news. Inside, I was devastated.

Hopefully, the limpid vision and jubilant images of Laurie's 1959 masterpiece *Cider with Rosie* will carry on delighting new readers for generations. His characters Cabbage-Stump Charlie, the local bruiser, Albert the Devil, the deaf mute beggar, and Percy-from-Painswick are his legacy.

A short distance from Stroud, he left another. One less known, and, possibly, dreamed up within the thick honey-coloured stonewalls and mullioned windows of the *Butchers Arms* in Sheepscombe where Laurie was once a regular bar snuggler.

The pub's iconic, carved sign depicts a struggling pig tethered to the leg of a blue-striped aproned, curly mopped chap, summoning up Dutch courage for turning pig into pork, staring into a frothy tankard of ale. Who's to say Laurie, a great cricket lover, didn't need lesser fortification having parted with £600 in 1968 for the far more agreeable task of buying the bent and buckled local cricket pitch.

His deed ensured the crack of leather on willow would reverberate in perpetuity through the Stroud valleys.

To play at Sheepscombe Cricket Club's 'Laurie Lee Field' is to enjoy cricket on the roof of the county. Here, only a brave man might suggest the bonkers contours would be better suited to cheese rolling or cross-country skiing. Should the spirit be willing but Shanks's pony be weak, a 4 x 4 is a the advisable method of negotiating the twisting goat track of Far End Lane that leads to where the field stretches out, in the author's words, like a pony's back. The pavilion is sited between its ears. The wicket occupies a hanging plateau where the saddle might be. And the boundary slope plunges over the animal's hindquarters into a spectacular gorge.

This is a place though not without its superstition. And there's talk of a ghost, and that's not just from Silly mid-on. It's said, the groundsman risks eternal damnation if he disturbs plantains or dandelions sprouting on what Frank Mansell, a legendary local fast bowler, who'd hurled his athletic frame up the escarpment for twenty-five years until his bones cried out for mercy, would have considered a good length.

Frank, a part-time poet whose day job was mending telephone lines for the GPO, was a kindred spirit and close friend of Laurie's. And he thought it fitting to immortalise Frank in *Cider With Rosie*: 'at first only the outfield was visible, then you'd see the top of Frank's cap. Then his flushed face and great heaving shoulders until gradually, like a galleon, he'd come billowing into view and loose his fast, furious ball like a shot from a cannon.'

On Frank's death in 1979, Laurie donated a brass plaque inscribed with the words 'In Sheepscombe let me lie.' It was screwed to a wooden bench on the top boundary. During the close season when nobody in his right mind would tackle the goat track the plaque was inexcusably nicked. But the plot thickened. Not only the plaque disappeared. One of Sheepscombe's revered trophies, featuring the remains of a stump Frank once shattered during a particularly brutish spell against neighbouring Birdlip, had gone with it.

Come 2003, Tony Francis of the *Daily Telegraph* investigated. He didn't learn much. 'You have only to mention Frank's name around the village and the conversation stops dead,' he wrote. What Tony did unearth, however, shed some light on an enigma. Laurie and Frank met one night at the Woolpack in Slad and struck up an almost instant friendship. Laurie helped his fellow wordsmith to publish his first collection of verse, which they delivered in cardboard boxes to rough-cider taverns up and down the valley. They shifted 2,000 copies of Cotswold Ballads in a week.

These days you can't get an edition of Frank's poetry for love nor money. Tony deduced, Frank simply became collectible, leaving Laurie's eulogy seeming truer than ever: 'the spirit of Frank Mansell won't leave Sheepscombe. He sits on that bench barracking the players when they do idiotic things. He never forgave bad play. Frank's unforgiving phantom, champion man that he was, is on that seat watching every move they make.'

This means he probably observed my Uncle Tubby, who, in attempting Frank's same furious steep gradient run up, came to a halt, hands on knees, knackered before his delivery stride.

So, let's just say, Tubby was one of Laurie's lesser pub acquaintances. Ever a bachelor to cricket, Tubby was christened 'Gervais'. As the name might suggest, he was born into the landed gentry, and with an entry in *Burke's*, Tubby, ever the gentlemen, could only ever have played first class cricket as an 'amateur'. That is if he had been really good with willow or leather. Which to be fair, despite being ever so keen, he wasn't. Perhaps it was down to size.

The nickname 'Tubby' followed his penchant for Old Gloucester Spot pork pies. And the family noticed, long before I had grown into my first pair of hobnailed cricket boots, the closest thing to fruit he ever deigned to eat was the orange of double Gloucester.

Nor was he helped by a sweet tooth, once remarking that if cut open he would be like a stick of rock candy with the word 'Gloucestershire' running all the way through him from top to toe.

Artistic and eccentric, he had dedicated his best efforts to the Shire. This first came to my attention in the age when the amateur cricketer wore his nylon work shirt to play, and umps in white coats had the look of ice cream salesmen about them.

Once, from the bottom of his ancient battered school truck, Tubby produced a home-made worse-for-wear mask closely resembling W.G. Grace. 'Just acrylic paint, cardboard, scissors, and elastic. I put the mask on for a bet once when I went out to bat for the village,' he boasted. 'It gave me confidence until the wretched elastic snapped scaring the shit out of a passing gull.'

I could only guess at the comments of the close fielders.

Tubby claimed to have also made a mask of Wally Hammond, but had 'got the spacey teeth all wrong' and it looked like an 'apparition from Halloween'. Swearing blind that the gruesome thing had been chucked away 'in the dim and distant past' he then offered to make me a mask of Mike Proctor.

'Nah, honestly. Thank you, but I'm fine. Really, don't bother.' I had blustered my refusal, trying not to hurt his feelings; especially as Tubby had the kind habit of giving me tickets to a few 'important' matches. As luck and Proctor would have it these turned out to be very fine matches, indeed.

And, for reasons it's best not to go into, he tended to suffer misfortunes that caused him to be disowned as the black sheep of the family. He only made matters worse for himself when he decided to live in a blue Bertram Hutchings caravan built around the time Sir Derrick Thomas Louis Bailey, 3rd Baronet, DFC stood down from the Shire captaincy. That's to say, the early 1950s.

Under Sir Derrick the Shire gave *Wisden* cause to cite a 'lack of batting solidity' as a reason why success wasn't achieved. The gurt tome, however, did offer a small amount of praise: 'a point to be remembered was that Gloucestershire almost invariably tried to play attractively. Sometimes they were beaten when risking all to win. To strike the balance between enterprise and match-winning cricket is not always easy'.

And Bailey was exonerated from criticism on his personal lack of solidity: 'Bailey's defensive stubbornness was worth more than its numerical value.'

Tubby would begin to impart the virtues of straight bat obduracy to me, more than a decade later, in the shadow of the caravan he called 'Aggy' - a name arising from the memory of a wartime girlfriend who 'worried about her eggs'.

Aggy, though, wasn't the only 'old girl' in Tubby's life. He shared Aggy with Polly, a ferociously jealous parrot dining on bananas-sprouts-asparagus-and-human blood.

An early forerunner of today's overseas influx, Tubby's 'lovely girl' was an African Grey acquired very much on impulse between cricket seasons after the couple had met in the German town of Munchengladbach. A sherry too many drunk to ward off the bitter winter chill was to blame. Whether that was by my uncle or by Polly, Tubby never confided.

As an honorary psittacine of the Shire Polly had been religiously taught by Tubby to scream 'GLAWSTER!', as a general statement, and in her twilight years 'Izzat Milton?'. The questionable squawk had nothing to do with Tubby's being able to recite passages from *Paradise Lost.* Instead, the sound was uttered only when the postman called.

The reason for this is explained by the esteem in which Tubby had held the late Bristolian Arthur Milton.

A slender fair-haired man, ever boyish in appearance and unruffled by nature, Arthur was the postman who holds the accolade of being the last footballer and cricketer to represent England in both sports. He spent his winters playing for Arsenal and Bristol City as a midfielder, and his summers taking the field for the Shire. And given what an amazing catcher of the cricket ball he was, he surely wouldn't have been half bad in goal.

After early mentoring from George Emmett the martinet, and Jack Crapp of bulldog semblance and the first-ever Cornishman to play for England, Arthur blessed the Shire with his presence for twenty-six years. Only Wally Hammond and Alf Dipper completed more centuries for the county. Indeed, when Wally first saw Arthur he said: "He'll do - but don't try to change him.' It was sound advice. He passed 1,000 runs in a season 16 times, scoring more than 32,000 first class runs at an average of 33, making his six Test appearances between 1958 and 1959.

David Green who had joined Gloucestershire from Lancashire as a player in 1968 held a particular memory of Arthur. One day at Old Trafford in 1965 Arthur was proving himself a nuisance. Tommy Greenhough's leg-spinners and googlies had Arthur either chasing smoothly up the pitch or moving quickly back over his stumps. David recalled Tommy muttering: 'I'm getting sick of the sight of Art down there, wandering about at t'back of his blade!' To David's trained eye, 'wandering about' was what it looked like. And he would later write: 'For such was Arthur's balance and ease of movement that he performed, with the most casual air, manoeuvres that in other players would have looked desperately risky.'

Ten year years after winning his first test cap he was awarded the county captaincy but with no great success. 'It was ten years too late when I was past my best as a player, ' he had wistfully lamented. 'One season in charge was quite enough.'

Arthur always liked to poddle along at his own pace. And in retrospect he put that down to the turgid Nevil Road track that he called his own 'tump'. Confiding with the *Guardian's* David Foot he said, 'I'm sure I'd have been a better player on another ground. My pal Tom Graveney's move to Worcester was the making of him.'

One or two of the powers–that-be suggested that Arthur might be a useful Test 'observer', and he was sent talent spotting in the south west and Wales. After filing many a detailed report about players' potential, he eventually grumbled, 'Frankly, I don't think they took a blind bit of notice, so I stopped doing it.'

In the Spring of 2007 Arthur's obituary appeared in the *Guardian*. David Foot described him 'generous with that calculated time-to-spare stroke off the back foot, who could win matches for his county while recoiling from any expansive style at the crease.'

But Tubby's real pull towards Arthur came from the latter being ever the dreamer and homespun philosopher. 'I loved the quiet of the early morning, looking at the stars,' Arthur once said, his sporting days over, choosing instead to get up before dawn to ride through Bristol Downs mists, thriving on a postman's work. 'People used to say I'd missed the big money of present-day sport. I told them I was still a millionaire, out on my bike as life stirred so excitingly.'

Oh, how Tubby empathized, always up with the dawn chorus he would fling open Aggy's battered door to the elements and let the breeze blow away the cobwebs, not to mention the tumbleweeds of fluff and feather that lay dormant on the floor during the stillness of night.

With Polly still in the land of nod he would practice his cricket strokes with a stick of celery while the kettle boiled, whispering to himself: 'C'mon Tubs, just two to win.' Then, with a flamboyant swing, he'd exclaim: 'The Shire's won! The Shire's won! Oh, what a match! Oh my, oh my!'

'GLAWSTER!' shrieked the woken bird.

The dull grey heads at family gatherings 'sans Tubby' opined that there was obviously something in the Stroud water. Why else, they asked, would any man of 'breeding' want behave like a bohemian? Cue a nervous titter from the maiden aunt.

To me, however, Tubby was ever the creative genius. With Aggy's plywood side panels representing wicketkeeper and slips Tubby set up a wicket. In front of the stumps, and with the aid of an old school easel, he propped a wooden paneled door that long ago had rotted off its hinges. At its bottom was a cat-flap. 'Think of the door as W.G.' he would say, 'and try and bowl the colossus through the gate.'

And whereas Arthur Milton used his bike as a vehicle of transport, Tubby's robust boneshaker was employed as my batting target. Hitting it with a stroke off the back foot 'Arthur Milton style' was worth four runs.

Between door and bike, endless hours of frustration and the lucky moments of insurmountable joy ensued, not mattering whether it was amongst the blooming of primroses or in the drizzle of Christmastide.

Cricket seasons melded. Polly in her dotage got a taste for KFC Hot Wings, and Aggy leaned toward the organic. Moss grew on the outside, damp cherry pattern wall paper peeled on the inside. By the time Tubby, with the help of a windfall inheritance from the maiden aunt, claimed twinges of arthritis, swopped celery stick for Brasher stick, and Aggy for a nondescript bungalow squatting a hefty heave from Cranham, Shire sap oozed in my veins.

A Much Told Story

During his England playing days Jack Crapp was room sharing with one of the Bedser twins. After last orders and probably a mite guddled, he returned late one evening to the hotel foyer to ask for his key. Before he could verbalise his request the receptionist asked, 'Bed, sir?'

'No, Crapp,' retorted Jack, and was promptly guided in the direction of the 'gents'.

Copperplate and Artful Toad

'Fellow citizens, we cannot escape history.'
Abraham Lincoln.

For my friend Goose, whose long neck added height to short leg, having a job cutting the grass for the rich little old ladies of Stroud had its perks. The best of these was time off.

'Hey, Somerset 12 Gloucester 7,' said Goose absorbing some data from his tablet.

'Rugby score?' I replied, not really concentrating.

'Nope. Wooden spoons.'

The coffee was expensive in the salubrious wifi hotspot. Wrinkling his nose up at cappuccino froth, Goose was trying to cheer himself up. More than any caffeine kick, the Shire ending up bottom of the County Championship on fewer occasions than Zum gave him a sudden high. One I quickly deflated.

'Let's hope it's not 12 – 8 in the short-term future. S'pose we must continue putting our faith in the Irish.' I didn't mean Goose's Irish girlfriend Mona having to find a better paid occupation. She, bizarrely, had gone to the same school in Northern Ireland as myself. Not that I'm really Irish. The school was just a happening of fate.

However, the recent influx of Irishmen into West Country cricket – William Porterfield, Kevin O'Brien, Hamish Marshall by default, and even George Dockrell of Zum - is something in which your author can take comfort, a way of connecting the past. As Goose lost himself again to his tablet, I sunk into disjointed memories.

Neither Dad or Mum identified the purpose, to me, of the pair of dusty, Dad-sized, studded, heavy soled clodhoppers, their grass stains daubed over with whitening, pushed to the back of the cloakroom shoe rack. They were a conundrum during my formative years spent growing up in Lisburn, the Northern Irish whiskey making town.

Then one summer, when I was six-ish, I saw a man in white hit a ball mightily using something thicker than a hurling stick from the middle of the town's park. A lot of other men in white stood and watched. Puzzled, I asked Mum what they were doing. 'Playing cricket', she said. 'It's very boring. Once there was a doctor with a beard as big as Father Christmas' who was famous for playing it.'

'Are they all doctors?' I asked, still absorbed by the men in white.

Mum said she didn't know. Neither did she hint that the robust, combative Englishman she referred to was as mythical as Santa, or that cricket was also played in England, where my family was shortly to move. Ferried away, Dad said, from the mash of cereal grains to where there was a mash of apples. And, more mysteriously, 'opportunity.'

Our arrival wasn't for the squeamish. Preparing the family reunion, Mrs Budd, my Nan's cook, crouched under a kitchen garden apple tree, a frantic hen struggling in the crook of her arm. With a swoosh of her cleaver she lopped off the bird's head. Like those static fielders in Ireland, I gawped, rooted to the spot, immobile, being where I shouldn't have been, as the creature's legs continued to run the three-minute mile.

The Sunday lunch table, however, quite put that early morning's gory apparition to the back of my mind. The laid out spread of roast chicken, stuffing and roast garden vegetables had me salivating. 'Let's say Grace,' said my Grandpa, piously.

'Let's say Grace scored a double hundred,' said my Dad, and beamed around the table. Despite related frowns, I grinned back at him, although not quite knowing why.

It was, I believe, the first mention of the great WG I had heard. Indeed, it was the first cricketing reference I ever had heard Dad sweeten my ears with. For all I knew 'Grace' could have been the name of some lady he knew. Little did I know my cricket education was beginning.

'If there's one sport that embodies Englishness, boy, it's cricket,' pontificated Dad.

Sat at that table, timid enquiry gleaned that Doctor William Gilbert Grace was the greatest player ever. His tall, bearded, wide-girthed figure earned him the nickname the 'Big 'Un'.

'Grace once played at Lansdown,' said Dad, knowingly.

Here was something I did know about. Although not sure ever hearing that cricket was played at the home of Irish rugby, I got excited. 'The Doctor played at Lansdowne Road. Wow!'

'No you silly boy, Lansdown Cricket Club, the MCC of the West. It's in Bath. And that's in an English county called Somerset.

I sifted the gobbledygook. 'Is Bath wetter than Ireland?'

After moving smoothly into becoming a nitwit, I learned some more geography. There was somewhere called Gloucestershire.

Later, I would realise, Lansdown was a cricket a club with a very big, facility rich clubhouse. In order to afford to play for the club chaps had to earn their keep. Some might have given a penny for the thoughts of Smokey aka Sir Vivian Richards, assistant groundsman, as he pushed the pitch roller, blisters on his hands. And whatever may have crossed his mind, he was flattening hallowed ground once the haunt of not only a teenage W.G., but also of his very bright brothers– the coroner Edward Mills known by his initials as E.M., and Fred. Their papa, Henry, a country doctor, had played cricket, and their mother loved the game. And with Henry making up numbers, W.G. and his brothers reputably took all the wickets at Lansdown between them, and probably never gave any inkling of coming off.

That said, it was across the border in Gloucestershire where the Big 'Un, E.M. and Fred rose to dizzy heights. In 1874, at Sheffield, W.G. and Fred between them took every Yorkshire wicket that fell to the bowlers in both innings. W.G. scored 167, and took 11 wickets. Fred scored 30, and took 6 wickets; the Shire beating Yorkshire by an innings and 94 runs.

It was W.G., though, who was the one off. Without him it was doubtful whether the popularity of cricket would have spread the way it did. Indeed, he appeared to symbolize the very rise of the English middle classes. Unsurprising, then, that he also captained England at Bowls.

Clever types will say that the introduction of the steam train and wider expansion of the railway network meant that the game of cricket could tour the country. All the Big 'Un had to do was hop aboard. An afternoon's work meant play in a benefit match, score a century, delight the crowd, and then put in a bill.

The Big 'Un alone could pull a crowd like no man. Despite his large frame and love of a good meal he had extraordinary stamina, and a will to win. He was a one off. He played as an amateur and made more money than any professional, putting appearance money down to 'expenses'.

To quote Simon Rae, author of *W.G. Grace - A Life*: 'You couldn't argue with W.G.. It was rather like the Titanic arguing with the iceberg. There could only be one winner. He was totally inflexible.'

On a visit to Somerset's Cricket Museum, a few decades after 'getting down' from the 'headlesss chicken' dinner table, I spied a lonely cricket ball – a battered looking sphere exhibited in a glass cabinet. The card written in faded copperplate alongside the ball was thin in detail: 'Ball presented by W.G. Grace to A. Bagley – Somerset v. Gloucestershire, 1897. Somerset bowled out for 57 in an hour.'

The distraction of the Big 'Un's presence on the field of play might have been the X factor in Zum's capitulation, although his actual contribution wasn't exactly awe-inspiring - 25 runs with the bat, and a solitary catch. The mere fact W.G. had touched the ball created its souvenir value. And he must practically have insisted on giving it to 'A. Bagley', a fervent Zum supporter. Certainly Sammy Woods, Zum's captain that day, was having nothing to do with W.G.'s celebrity, preferring instead to call him 'an artful old toad'.

Yet it would seem WG's generous donation was true to character; well, certainly according to the late 19th century sports journalist Arthur Porritt, who just happened to be the Big 'Un's ghost writer. 'About Doctor W.G. Grace, there was something indefinable,' he wrote. 'A wonderful kindness ran through his nature, mingling strangely with the arbitrary temper of a man who's been accustomed to be dominant over other men.'

Not given to doing post-match interviews W.G. was never very forthcoming on his feelings during the 44 years in which he played 880 games of cricket, the last being in 1908 against the Gentleman of England. So it was always down to others to collect the tasty snippets that when put together presented the gurt man as being ruddy fantastic. Gleaning such stuff wasn't a cake-walk.

Annoyingly, great players, those the public really want to hear from, are rarely prone to analysing their gifts. Porritt, for instance, was continually exasperated. 'Getting material from Grace,' he said, 'was almost heartbreaking. All he would say in recording some dazzling feat of his was "then I went in and made 284".'

I had wondered to myself whether W.G. had any failings. Forgetfulness might have been one. A picture of him hanging at Lords shows him in cricket whites but with brown brogues on his feet. Had he forgotten to change his footwear before posing?

For me to dissemble myth from fact I needed a convenient place to start. The task was to find somebody who had the grey cells required. The clue as to who that might be was in the quality of handwriting beside the Victorian Zum ball.

Only one person I'd heard of had copperplate anywhere near as good. He was a bloke who had been the Shire's first team scorer for an age, and whose scorebooks were absolutely immaculate. So detailed were they that you could 'read stories out of them'.

This wasn't my opinion. Rather it was that of a cricketing son of Chipping Sodbury, Graham Wiltshire. I had bustled into the medium-fast old 'un as he busied himself organizing his own testimonial. It had been Graham who'd put me onto the trail of the only scorer he'd ever known who 'scored with a pen'. He wasn't talking about football, but of real fountain ink, no biro. And about good old-fashioned English handwriting.

I headed for the cricket museum at Nevil Road. There I would find the curator of his own wonderful creation. That is, if he wasn't in the bar. Unfortunately, he was in neither.

Outside, still searching of the elusive gentleman, I poddled straight into a Shire training session led by former batsman-cum-wicketkeeper, Andy Stovold. In the middle of Nevil Road's cricket square, Andy put it simply: 'Bert Avery is Gloucestershire. If you can't find him, he'll be having his daily flutter on the horses.'

True to form, I caught up with Bert as he was stuffing a couple of fivers into his pocket prior to adjusting his smart tie. A man in his late 70s with a receded hairline, tooth sparse gums suggested a need for dentures. His eyes smiled through wide thick lens glasses as the laughter lines of age creased his face, playing around the corners of a slightly protruding bottom lip.

When it came to Shire cricket, what Bert didn't know wasn't worth knowing. And I had my Moleskine at the ready as we found a quiet corner of the museum to chat. Any of the four corners would have done.

He had seen Andy Stovold through almost the whole of his cricketing career in the first team. Neither of them had ever won very much on the gee-gees, but they had shared great times over the years.

'I got interested in cricket from about 8-years old, really.' he confided. 'When I'm not here you'll find me at my local club, Shirehampton.

'That's very appropriate for you, isn't it? I said, allowing myself a chuckle. 'what with their home being in Penpole Lane.'

'Never thought of that,' Bert snorted before lowering his voice to a whisper. 'I will say this – before I came up to Gloucestershire to watch and to score for the county I'd seen more Somerset matches. I had a Grandmother that lived at Bridgwater, and I used to spend all my holidays down at Taunton. And an uncle was head of the Taunton gatemen, so it didn't used to cost me anything to go in and sit on the old benches there. It was 1965 when I came to the notice of Gloucester.'

I didn't push him on his loyalties. Instead, I broached the subject of W.G.

Bert took to it like a duck to water. What followed almost became a monologue. 'The good doctor? Where do I start? He simply bestrode the cricket scene, and it's said between he and Prime Minister Gladstone it was touch and go who was the better known in England, or the nation at large.'

Raising an index finger to point at the ceiling, Bert carried on seamlessly. 'Once, playing at the Ship Field for Thornbury, his brother E.M.'s village team, he was caught off a wall and refused to 'walk'. It caused the club to bring in the rule that the ball had to be hit out of the ground for a six. Another time, he was given out first ball and he said to the ump, "I'm not out. They didn't come here to you give me out. They came to see me bat." Mind you he didn't always get away with such audacity. In his second innings in the first ever Test match against Australia in 1880 he faced two balls, and was out for 0.

'All three Grace brothers were in that England side. It's a sad thing, but Fred Grace died of pneumonia from a chill caught whilst waiting at Reading Station, two weeks after getting a pair. However, the story goes, and it's long before my time, that if he had been alive he'd probably have exceeded W.G.'s feats.

'Did you know, W.G. ran as a hurdler for England during a Test match?'

'No. That's amazing,' I said.

'Yep, he left the match and went across to the White City, took part in the race, won it, then came back and continued playing the game. And, I think, he scored a century, as well.

'You just mention W.G. to probably anybody, like some dear old dowager duchess, and they'd know you meant W.G. Grace. He was cricket. Any cricket club you go to has a picture of the old boy there, and like as not he'd never been to some of 'em. He's just been a legend in his lifetime. And that's all there is to it. You hear many stories about the man.

'One time, a ball lodged in his shirt as he was batting. And he kept running up and down the wicket with someone chasing him trying to get the ball out.' Bert burst into a fit of laughter that left him wheezing.

'Not many people know this one,' he said having calmed down, 'W.G. once declared the innings closed very unexpectedly when he himself had made 93 not out. And he came back to the pavilion and a member said, "Doctor, very surprising you decided to declare. Why did you do that?" And the great man said, "that's because 93 is the only score between 0 and 100 that I've never yet made."'

I had to ask Bert's two most 'telling' anecdotes. This got him rubbing his chin.

'August 1885, Clifton,' said Bert after a prolonged silence. 'After sitting up all night attending on a bad maternity case, The doctor carried his bat through an innings of 348, scoring 221; then took six wickets for 45, and in the Middlesex follow-on got five for 75.

'But that wasn't the best.' Now, I paraphrase Bert's words. Clifton was merely the encore to what had happened ten years before at Gravesend. There, W.G. scored 257 out of 443 before being last out on the Saturday. Then after lunch Kent were dismissed for 76. Of the 106 runs which gave Gloucestershire victory by nine wickets W.G. scored 73, while to complete the remarkable three days, during which he was on the field while every ball was bowled, he trotted from the dressing tent in his tweed tail suit and hard felt hat, carrying his heavy cricket bag to a four-wheeled cab which took him to the station.

The thought of Gravesend brought a quote by A.A. Thompson to mind. He was moved to write: 'what do I think of W.G.? Why, I have never seen his like and never shall. I tell you my opinion, which is that W.G. should never be put underground. When he dies his body ought to be embalmed and permanently exhibited in the British Museum as "The colossal cricketer of all time".'

Having once asserted, 'I don't like blocking; you only get three,' only four balls passed the doctor's bat during W.G.'s hundredth hundred at Bristol in 1895. Each of the four was counted and committed to memory by the Honorary Canon Archdale Wickham, Zum's gauntleted stumper. The Big 'Un celebrated his achievement with champagne so revitalising that he proceeded on to make 288 in three hundred and twenty minutes.

A lavish dinner, a black bow tie affair to which I had the privilege to be invited, was thrown by Gloucestershire to celebrate the centenary of the great event.

Goose, his grande cappuccino now cold, drew me abruptly out of my reverie. 'Bugger the Irish, what the Shire needs is a return to Grace,' he exclaimed.

Harsh, but he must have been reading my thoughts. Yet, if a Thornbury pedigree was needed one could, perhaps, forget about Grace and, instead, place faith in the somewhat slighter figure of Chris Dent.

Excerpt
'Grace at Gloucester'

I saw the 'Old Man' once
When he was old and I
Was young. He did not score.
So far as I recall, a heap of runs
Nor even hit a four.
But still he lives before my schoolboy eye
A giant among pygmies. In his hand.
The bat looked like a toy. I saw him stand
Firm set on legs as massive as the piers
Of the Norman nave at Gloucester; and the cheers
Which greeted him on the 'Spa' where heard
As far as the Cathedral. When he stirred
The ground shook, and the crazy old
Pavilion creaked and groaned.

Upon the Spa no county players pace;
The great ones of to-day it does not know,
I deem it better so.
Leaving the elm-girt field its dreams of Grace.

Oscar Lloyd.

1878 saw the Shire's first match against Lancashire. Taking place at Old Trafford the match generated a huge fervour. 16,000 came in huge crocodiles of humanity through the four official gates while another 2,000 didn't even bother to queue barge and simply clambered over the boards. The game itself was the inspiration for cricket's best-known poem, and it was written by a 19-year-old.

At Lord's

It is Glos'ter coming North, the irresistible,
The Shire of the Graces, long ago!
It is Gloucestershire up North, the irresistible,
And new-risen Lancashire the foe!
A Shire so young that has scare impressed its traces,
Ah, how shall it stand before all restless Graces?
O, little red rose, their bats are as maces
To beat thee down, this summer long ago!

This day of seventy-right they are come up North against thee,
This day of seventy-eight, long ago!
The champion of the centuries, he cometh up against thee,
With his brethren, every one a famous foe!
The long-whiskered Doctor, that laugheth rules to scorn,
While the bowler, pitched against him, bans the day that he was born:
And G.F. with his science makes the fairest length forlorn;
They are come from the West to work thee woe!

Francis Thompson.

Playing Fast and Loose

Robert Henry Kingscote, 1802-1882, was of the landed gentry and played for one of the earliest cricket teams in Gloucestershire. At 6' 6" he was a big chap and a mighty tonker. About him someone wrote:

'A fine slashing hitter as ever was found,
He sometimes hit the ball out of the ground:
An excellent thrower, a hundred yards clear,
And the ladies protest he runs like a deer.'

THREE

Long Whiskers and Kites

'Long whiskers cannot take the place of brains.'
Russian Proverb.

These days Frenchay is, perhaps, best known for its University campus. It was not always so.

The local hospital ballooned during World War II for the US Army, which treated the bloody mess of wounded soldiers returning from the D-Day Normandy landings. It may have been this that prompted a need for light relief among medical staff. To meet this end one needed look no further than young hospital doctors. They can be an eccentric and sporty bunch, earning a reputation for often letting their hair down.

One such set of medics, however, did not so much let their hair down, but attach it in charitable long whiskered celebration. The 'Frenchay Hospital W.G. Grace Team' took to the field to honour that local cricketing doctor of fulsome facial growth.

Among the cricket archives of Knowle West Media Centre is a set of black and whites photographs taken in 1980 on a day of shirtsleeves, summer frocks and picnic chairs. A team of medics in creams and whites posed in front of a little, white-painted, wooden pavilion slightly touched by rot. Each sported a false beard undoubtedly sourced from a fancy dress shop.

On making their way to the wicket, and with a ball carefully placed on a good length, five of their number arranged themselves as if to await the smoking powder flash of Victoriana. Surrounded by a slip, silly point, short leg and a crouching wicketkeeper, the batsman, his cap slightly askew, held the classic stance of a lower order rabbit. His vertical bat covered middle stump, but the gate left between bat and pads was as wide as the seat of W.G. Grace's trousers. The great man himself would have turned in his grave had he witnessed such technique. Though, any such turn might have become a somersault had he known this was poor mimicry of himself when captain of Frenchay Cricket Club, the oldest cricket club in Bristol and one of the oldest in the West Country.

Today, Frenchay is a Bristol suburb set between the M32, and the wooded River Frome valley, and the club plays at Hambrook alongside the Old Filton Road, having moved there in 1950 from its old home on the Frenchay Common.

The *'Frenchay Cricket Club - Centenary Book 1846–1946'* reads: '1870. Captain: W.G. Grace, Esq.' He was 21, and he joined Gloucester County Cricket Club the same year. His days at Lansdown were memory. The captaincy of Frenchay was a natural progression as W.M., W.G.'s elder brother, who'd joined in 1862, was skipper before him although EM had joined even earlier, in 1861.

But, what was it that so attracted the three of them? Frenchay was first recorded in 1257 as 'Fromscawe', meaning the wood on the Frome. Purely, it seems, for the sake of interest, the book gives an insight into the south Gloucestershire geography of the local cricket pitch that the Grace brothers would have known so well:

'Through the village, at the top of the slope north, is the small green plateau on the east side on which is the church. The green was practically covered with trees – stately elms, horse chestnut, spreading sycamores and almost in front of the church, a line of four tall poplars.

'Quarrying has scarred the surface and had left its tumps and holes to mar and spoil the beauty of Frenchay Common. In such surroundings, among the trees, was a small, naturally flat space, and it was on this that the first cricket pitch was made in the early part of the nineteenth century.'

From what began beside those quarry tumps in 1846 commenced a steady proliferation of Gloucestershire cricket clubs. The club's founding came two years before the Big 'Un was born at Downend, a village too pitiful to raise a cricket team and one where, W.G. would observe, 'tourists, when they travelled that way, rarely paid it the compliment of staying long in it'.

As fate would have it, Downend was just a couple of miles, as the crow flies, from Frenchay Common. W.G.'s parents, Henry and Martha, had been married for seventeen years, having tied the knot just a few weeks after the Bristol Riots had devastated Bristol city centre.

Although, only by the Grace of God, were W.G. and his eight siblings ever born at all. Martha's dad, George Pocock, was an inventor of huge kites. Some were designed to pull carriages, and one, with the intrepid Martha strapped into an armchair, was flown up over the chasm of the Avon Gorge.

Much better that she got grandstand views of Frenchay cricket from her pony-trap. And from that vantage point she would undoubtedly have been witness to the home players imbibing in bottles of claret kindly supplied by one of the club's patrons.

Since those halcyon early days Frenchhay CC was closely connected with both the Shire and the Grace family, and, to a lesser degree, Somerset. By this I mean the county of Zum, and not, 'Colonel Somerset', another former club patron from when Frenchay virtually teamed Graces.

However, given the role of Graces in the club's history the *Centenary Book* makes a rather surprising assertion. 'Without question,' it states, 'Harry Smith was the finest all-round cricketer Frenchay ever produced. A player who it is safe to say will never be forgotten as long as cricket is played at Frenchay.'

Indeed, sport was in Harry's blood. Like Arthur Milton he was a first-class foot-baller, playing for First Division Bolton Wanderers until a serious injury ended his career early. Harry the cricketer remains a tad unsung. Unfortunately, his name is not one that springs readily to mind these days when it comes to a talented keeper of the gloves. So it's high time he's hailed with the credit he deserved. Especially when discovering he was once pronounced as being the best wicket-keeper in the country.

Little more than a boy from Fishponds Harry joined Frenchay as a bowler. Indeed, he became a fine one. Nor was he a mug with the bat. Village cricket proved a stepping-stone to achieving county status. He played many years for Glouces-tershire and also gained Test Match honours.

He was discovered by Gloucestershire in 1912 and eventually succeeded Jack Board as the county stumper. Against Hampshire at Southampton in 1919 he made 120 and 102 not out. *Wisden's Almanack* raises a noteworthy incident occur-ring in that match. Pothecary, the last Hampshire batsman, played a ball from Parker into the top of his pad, shook it into Smith's hands, and was given out caught contrary to 'Law 33 B' which declares in such a case that the ball becomes dead.

And he's on a par with Andy Wilson and Barry Meyer when it comes to wicket-keeping records by instigating six or more dismissals in an innings, an achieve-ment he attained against Sussex at Bristol in 1923. He snaffled a trio of catches and whipped off the bails for three adroit stumpings.

Cricket gurus, though, point to the 1927 season as probably being one of Harry's best. In four successive innings he allowed only one bye, while opponents compiled 1,374 runs for 23 wickets.

And Harry was the England selectors choice of wicky for the first Test Match against the West Indies at Lord's in 1928. Also in that England eleven was Harry's Shire teammate Wally Hammond. England won by an innings and 58 runs. Harry's contribution was scoring 7 and a first innings dismissal of Windies opener George Challenor, caught off the bowling of Larwood.

But for the fact that Bert Strudwick was at his best around this time Harry would surely have gained more Test caps. His ill-health came as a great blow to the county. Because of it he was unable to play at all in 1932, and though in 1935 he turned out again, he couldn't stand the strain. He was dead within two years aged just 46.

'Quiet and unassuming, always cheerful, and a thorough sportsman, Harry Smith has left a fragrant memory,' the club said. But when one thinks of the general state of a jobbing keeper's kitbag, 'fragrant' wasn't necessarily a compliment to draw attention.

Frenchay, on the other hand, attracted attention to itself once more in 1945. A fortnight after German forces in Berlin had surrendered to the Allies in May, Howard Marshall of the BBC commentated on Frenchay versus Stapleton on Frenchay Common. Normalcy returning to the village greens of England was the media point wanting to be made. And Frenchay, the village cricket team of the Grace family, was emphatically the obvious choice.

Certainly, it would appear, the doctors of Frenchay Hospital agreed the club's cricket history was something worth dressing up for. Might they have felt inclined to pay similar tribute to Harry Smith? Well, who's to say?

Presented Bats and a 'Graceful' Eight

After he broke the world triple jump record E.M. Grace dominated for Lansdown when they played Frenchay in 1861. In his diary he wrote: 'Presented with a bat for making 121 when the French had had enough of it and would not play further'.

In 1862 E.M. joined the Frenchay Club and was presented with a bat for making 208 not out against Knowle Park. The innings included 'some magnificent drives and leg hits, including one clean 8 and numerous others – a tremendous innings.

On another occasion he hit a ball just above the clock on Frenchay church.

Frenchay v. The Schoolmasters, 1871

Frenchay scored 133 (G.F. Grace 47) and the Schoolmasters 105. 'Remarks' in the scorebook read: 'Time for drawing stumps 6.15. The last man of the schoolmasters was in at 6.10 – the church clock was on the quarter – last over being given, and the last ball of all of the over took the wicket, thus deciding the game in favour of Frenchay.

'Some little unpleasantness occurred in this game arising from the somewhat slow manner in which the Schoolmasters appeared at the wicket after the fall of their predecessors' bails. Cricket should be cricket.'

A Daft Hint

At the back of Frenchay CC scorebook dating from 1897 are few cricketing hints written by a local fellow called Richard Daft. He describes one batting stroke as 'the under-leg stroke'. Used on many occasions in the past, perhaps, John Bracewell could reinvent it and give it a whirl at Gladiator net practice.

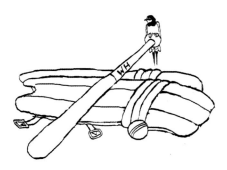

FOUR

Old Cocks and Swallow Snaffling

There's music in the names I used to know,
And magic when I heard them, long ago.

As I feel now to recall those lovely names
Jeweling the lov'liest of our English games.

Surely, the glow they held was the high sun's!
Or did a young boy's worship think it so,
And is it but his heart that's aching now?

Thomas Moult.

Behind his cricket museum's closed door Bert Avery had moved on from the subject of the Big 'Un. Indeed, he seemed to have left the topic of cricket altogether.

My brain reeled from a litany of shnuggets, those shared, bite-size pieces of information, which hold great value or significance and are greeted with surprise, pleasure and great interest. 'The Crecy Window in Gloucester Cathedral is the largest stained glass window in Britain,' Bert said, 'And of course, part of the M5 north of junction 13, the long, straight, wide bit, used to be a runway.'

Bert was playing games and I found myself fighting my low boredom threshold, my concentration slipping, despite the interesting exhibits behind the cricket museum's glass.

'Wally caught a swallow once. Well, reputedly.' Bert must have seen that he'd quickly regained my attention. He chuckled. 'Thought I'd lead up to throwing in that one to see of you were on the ball.'

'I'm rapt,' I said.

There followed a knock on the door, and in ambled the Bomber.

'I think we're talking about Wally Hammond,' I said to the newcomer, Bryan 'Bomber' Wells.

'Thought you would be,' said Bomber, smiling broadly, and speaking with his broad Gloucester vowels. 'Just came to add my tenpenny worth to Bert.' This might not be so great, I thought. Bomber had played for the Shire during Hammond's last match.

'Can I get on, Bryan?' twinkled Bert through his spectacles. 'Between the war years Wally was the greatest cricketer of his generation. Beginning his career in 1922, he played as a professional, but looked to the gentleman amateur for inspiration.

'1928 was his greatest year as an all-rounder. Just before he went on his wonderful tour of Australia, in the course of two matches in one week against Surrey and Worcestershire he was simply outstanding. Against Surrey he made a century in each innings and caught ten catches. In the two matches altogether he made 360 runs, and took 16 wickets and took 11 catches – an all round achievement in one week which can never have been bettered before or since.'

True, Bert, I thought. But in a toss up between the Surrey match and the one against Worcestershire, surely it was the latter at Cheltenham that was the more remarkable. Indeed, it was one of the most incredible performances ever seen in a first-class match. The pitch was of the awkward variety, and *Wisden* relates that Wally 'made the ball turn appreciably and swing through the air' as he took nine for 23 in the visitors' first innings of 35 all out. And with the pitch still problematic he made a majestic 80 and finally, on a surface magicked into friendliness, took six for 105 to bowl the Shire to victory by an innings.

Bomber felt the urge to contribute. 'Wally reserved his best shows of skill for after the crowds went home,' he chipped in. 'I remember when Kent came to play Gloucestershire at Bristol in the '30s. Tom Goddard bowled them out on a turning pitch in no time at all to win by an innings. Kent went home on the second day. Hammond came into the dressing room afterwards and said, "Tom, what are you so pleased about? They batted very badly. I could have played you with a stick of rhubarb." Wally was probably taking the micky.

"'Anyway," he said, "come out in the middle." And he got all the side out in the middle again and into their fielding positions after Kent had disappeared. And he got Tom to bowl to him on this worn pitch, and believe it or not, Wally played Tom Goddard with the edge of his bat on a turning pitch against a master of off spin.

'After that Wally played Charlie Parker and Ray Sinfield without any bother at all. Then he chucked his bat in the corner of the net and brought out his baseball bat. And he played the ball with that, belting the ball all over the place.

'And Charlie said, "I was so annoyed, I got this ball and instead of bowling it at him I threw it at him." And Wally calmly went 'Baaannggg!' And he hit the ball many a mile with the baseball bat. Wally went back into the pavilion and Charlie turned to all the players, and there were some great ones there, and he said, "Gentlemen, you've been honoured to have seen the greatest exhibition of batting you'll ever see in your life."'

Bert obvious thought it was time he said something. 'Wally never used a cross-bat stroke to a straight ball; except, perhaps, to a rank long-hop below medium pace, when he employed a lovely low sweep to leg with a horizontal bat. Nor did he ever seem to hook. A law unto himself, he would step back and force the short ball to the off, but not many men possessed such power of wrist and forearm, and quickness on the feet, to be able to do that.'

Wally, though, wasn't infallible. I knew this from an archive pointing to June 1927 and the incidence of missed chances at Taunton, a match Zum eventually escaped from with a draw.

Hammond had arrived fresh as a daisy having completed 1000 runs in May. Zum skipper Jack 'Farmer' White had been asked the previous day what chance he had of dismissing the world's greatest batsman. He replied, as was his style, 'I think we'll get that cock all right.' Keenly interested to see what Farmer could do to stop Hammond's prolific sequence of centuries, Major C.H.B. Pridham, a Zum supporter, planted himself in a seat directly behind the bowler's arm in the old pavilion. This is the Major's record of what happened:

'Hammond came in and started off in great style, reaching 40 without mishap. Then it was that White sent down a very slow and tempting delivery. The batsman went for it like a trout at a mayfly, running several yards out of his ground – and missed it completely; but alas, Dar Lyon the wicket-keeper failed to take the ball after many attempts, and Hammond got safely back. Again. Another twenty-odd runs scored in full confidence that the gods were with him after his lucky escape. Yet once more did White entice him out of his crease to miss the ball, and again did the stumper blunder, whilst we in our seats stifled sounds of distress.

'The great batsman then went his sweet way, complete master of the bowling until he got to 197. One more hit for his 200. It came, that hit at the ball, but this time White had his long-delayed revenge, and down went his wicket. The bowler had virtually taken Hammond's wicket three times that afternoon. All this time White had persevered and kept his head and length, though the stumper's blunders were enough to make cricket's angels weep.'

At no time did the Major mention that Dar Lyon's brother Bev was the Shire's wicky. How far did brotherly love go?

But whereas Dar hadn't covered himself in glory, Wally in the field was exemplary. Some even commented that his slip fielding to Farmer White in Test matches, and to Parker and Goddard of the Shire was absolute mustard.

And while on the subject of slippage it's worth mentioning a rather soggy Test match where Wally saved the day. Played in 1935 at the Oval, a ground referred to locally as 'The Mecca' of cricket, and also home to the Dickensian sounding Pickwick Cricket Club until 2005, I'm not talking about salvation in England's capital. No, this was all about the Kensington Oval west of Bridgetown, the capital city of Barbados.

The game was the first in a four Test series against the West Indies. England's shipper Bob Wyatt won the toss and inserted the opposition, in what turned out to be rather a strange, low scoring affair in which England declared their first innings on 81 for 7, still 21 runs behind the Windies first all out effort. By hitting 43, Wally Hammond had hit over half of England's runs without once managing a boundary over the squidgy outfield. Batting second time around the Windies declared on 51 for 6, confidently throwing down the gauntlet upon what had become a pernicious rain-affected pitch that showed no sign of easing. England needed 73, and Wally slid to the wicket with his side 5 down for 43.

He was to hit the only boundary of the whole match, a six, to bypass the puddles and squelch. And in finishing not out on 29, he brought England victory by 4 wickets. The tourists, though, when on to lose the series two to one, though they might have called 'foul!'in the fourth and deciding Test in Jamaica.

At the top of England's first innings a ball bowled by Windies bowler Manny Martindale copped Wyatt one in the chops. He was carried unconscious from the field with his jaw broken in four places. When he regained consciousness in the dressing room, his first action was to signal for a pencil and paper - when these were supplied he wrote down an amended batting order for his team. This was a chap who played for both Warwickshire and Worcestershire and shows the calibre of chap the Shire came up against in local derby games.

However, eleven years later, in 1946, when forty-two Wally was still, almost, at his very best, and topped the national averages. But by then, Dennis Compton had already taken Wally's mantle as England's greatest batsman.

Peter West told me the story of his only conversational encounter with Wally. It came in the flaming June of '46, and it's a cringe worthy tale, again from Taunton, that could be dredged from my own experiences of trying to gather material from household cricketing names.

Peter had been a cub agency reporter dispatched to gather details from Shire skipper Wally. One can only wonder at Peter's excitement in interviewing a cricketer he worshipped. Knocking on Wally's dressing room door on the last day of the match, Peter was invited to enter. And with a respect amounting to reverence, he said: 'Sir, my sports editor has asked if you can tell me your side for the next fixture.'

'F... off,' his hero replied.

A couple of months later, in the return fixture at Bristol on August Bank Holiday, and watched by a schoolboy David Allen amongst a crowd of about 18,000 souls, Wally made 214 before being caught by Micky Walford off Horace Hazell's slow left arm, a bloke who had been bowling his slow left-armers for Zum since 1929 and as a youngster had idolised his victim. The match was Wally's last appearance at Bristol until a disastrous comeback in 1951.

Sadly by then the Shire were in the doldrums. The post-war boom in attendances had ebbed away. The club needed a membership drive. Where better to start than August Bank Holiday Monday against Zum. And someone on the committee had the brain wave that if Wally could be persuaded to play then it would guarantee a full house.

Being realistic, the notion turned out less successfully than Sir Alex Ferguson recently bringing Paul Scholes out of football retirement for Manchester United.

With Wally Hammond agreeing to play, a capacity crowd did indeed flock on the Saturday to see the first day. The Shire batted and expectant spectators sat and waited for W.H. to walk to the crease. The players too felt a sense of awe.

Among them was Bomber Wells, then a 21-year-old Shire off-spinner who'd made his county debut a week or so earlier.

'All Gloucestershire people were weaned on Wally Hammond. And that was the standard we were expected to reach when I played here.' he reflected, casting a glance to Bert as if to seek agreement. 'If you could play you played, and if you couldn't then you got the sack.'

Bomber paused before continuing. Bert just looked sad, aware of what was coming.

'That match in '51,' said Bomber, 'was like standing in the presence of God. I can't describe it. Wally Hammond was such a legend. He was 48 and looking much older because of the way he'd looked after himself… or not looked after himself. He smiled and shook hands. And I realised what large hands he had, and his forearms were huge, like legs of pork.

'It was more than halfway through Saturday before the first wicket fell. Arthur Milton and George Emmett each scored a hundred in an opening stand of 193. Then two quick wickets fell and Hammond emerged from the pavilion to join Arthur. The crowd rose as one to cheer him all the way to the middle. But the Wally they were anticipating was only a memory.'

Even I knew the rest. David Foot would write in his biography *Wally Hammond - The Reasons Why*: 'There was no longer any majesty in his walk to the crease. The flannels were immaculate as ever but the limbs were weary, and it couldn't be hidden.'

From the moment he faced his first ball - surviving a loud ell bee appeal - it was clear Wally's comeback was a ghastly mistake. He could barely put willow on leather. And when he did, Arthur later noted: 'he was cursing quietly as he mistimed balls he once hammered.' In the Shire dressing room the players turned away dismayed. Tom Graveney, in his fourth season with the county, just sat inside the pavilion. 'I couldn't watch any of it,' he reportedly said.

After 50 sad minutes Wally came down the track and was bowled by Horace Hazell. He had managed seven singles. Horace finished with 8 for 102 but Hammond's was the wicket he wanted. 'I owed that bugger that one,' he told former Zum player turned journo Eric Hill years later.

Bert broke an awkward silence by clearing his throat. 'In his prime, Hammond topped the national averages, in 1933, '34, '35, '36, '37, '38, and '39. Then, after his six years in the forces, he came back to top them again, of course, in 1946. No other player came even close to surpassing him until the arrival of Zaheer Abbas, the Pakistan Test cricketer.'

Bert and Bomber decided it was time for a bar break. And they left me to my thoughts on Zed.

Dubbed the 'Asian Bradman', and a chap who in Peter West's opinion destroyed attacks with 'a flashing rapier', Zed joined the county in 1972. He stayed for thirteen seasons.

Alastair Hignell, Zed's team-mate for the best part of ten years, put flesh on a legend by describing him as 'bespectacled, studious and mild-mannered, (and) seemed more like a check-in clerk at Pakistan International Airways than the star player for their cricket team.'

'Skinny, frail and allergic to strenuous exercise Zed was a reluctant fielder and couldn't see the point of taking more than two paces to deliver his apologetic offspin.'

He hated the chill of England, but not as much as his compatriot and Shire team-mate Sadiq Mohammad. The latter went out to field one icy April afternoon wearing his pyjamas under his tracksuit under his whites. And although Zed disliked the daily grind of the county cricket circuit, blimey, could he bat.

Alastair observed, for all Zed's single-minded concentration, he had a thing about records. After a double-century at Canterbury, Zed seemed to realise that he would miss out on a second-innings century if Alastair scored too many of the runs required for victory and, marching down the wicket, ordered him to block.

And there were further questions about Zed's ego. In his testimonial year Zed, coming across as shy and as unassuming as he looked, asked Alastair to help him write letters to potential benefactors. The problem was he was as reluctant to turn out in benefit games as he was to make personal appearances. Alastair asked him how he proposed to 'secure some of their largesse.'

'Just say I am the best batsman in the world,' Zed answered. 'That should be good enough'. Indeed, a Pakistani newspaper reported that Zed, and Sadiq for that matter, had been given a rare honour by the Shire. Two villages, it was claimed, had been renamed after them by 'suffixing their first names to them in recognition of their services to the County'. Where that particular story originated remains a mystery.

When the Shire capped Zed in 1972 most of W.G.'s and W.H.'s batting records looked unassailable. But, neither of those two managed a double-century and a hundred in the same match. Zed managed it four times. In all, he was unbeaten in eight innings. Wally managed the feat on seven occasions. So Zed's achievements were truly amazing. In 206 matches for the Shire Zed scored more than 16,000 runs at just under 50, a phenomenal return when one considers the County Championship matches only lasted three days, that there was a 100-over limit on each first innings, and, like Wally Hammond, he didn't open the batting.

But most of all, what Zed did better than Wally, was to know when to retire.

A Photograph of Hammond

Even at 1/500th you can't freeze him
Makes his image quite static,
He remains more mobile than diagrammatic.

Take compass, protractor. However
You dismantle him, the parts
Remain true, suggest velocity.

Leonardo would have made him fly,
This batsman so revving with power
He seems airborne.

Like some prototype birdman
Straining at silk moorings, he conveys
Ambiguity, both imprisonment and release

Never mind the earthbound heaviness
Of hip, of shoulders, his cover-drive
Evokes airiness, and effortless take-off.

A study in anatomy, circa 1930. Anonymous.
But there, nonchalantly stuffed
In his pocket, that blue handkerchief signs it.

Alan Ross

Gentlemen v. Players
Lord's, 17th and 18th July, 1946.
A prime example of the vagaries of cricket

The Players had declared their innings closed at 399 for loss of 5 wickets. The Gentlemen replied to this with 138 for the loss of 5 wickets, but their last 6 wickets fell for 6 runs; following on, their first 5 wickets fell for 6 runs – 11 wickets in succession thus falling for 15 runs. Six of them – including Hammond – were dismissed without scoring a run. As every one of the Gentlemen's XI were involved in this collapse, the whole side were virtually dismissed for 15 runs, though this was completed in the follow-on. One can truly never tell what will happen next, in this weird, eccentric and curious game of cricket.

Wally Hammond's Finest Match

GLOUCESTERSHIRE v WORCESTERSHIRE
County Championship 1928.
College Ground, Cheltenham on 18th, 20th August 1928 (3-day match)
Worcestershire won the toss and elected to bat
Umpires W Bestwick, HI Young

Worcestershire first innings

*JB Higgins		b Hammond	2
L Wright	st Smith	b Hammond	8
BW Quaife	c Hammond	b Parker	2
WV Fox	c Lyon	b Hammond	1
HHIH Gibbons	c Stephens	b Hammond	4
CF Root	c Seabrook	b Hammond	0
CV Tarbox		b Hammond	6
JW King	not out		0
JJ Bowles	c Lyon	b Hammond	4
DV Hill	c Parker	b Hammond	0
+FT Summers		b Hammond	0
Extras (5 b, 3 lb)			8
Total (all out, 20.2 overs)			35

Fall of wickets:
1-8, 2-15, 3-19, 4-19, 5-19, 6-24, 7-31, 8-35, 9-35, 10-35 (20.2 ov)

Gloucestershire bowling	Overs	Mdns	Runs	Wkts
Hammond	10.2	2	23	9
Sinfield	2	1	3	0
Parker	8	7	1	1

Gloucestershire first innings

AE Dipper	c Quaife	b Wright	77
RA Sinfield	c Hill	b Wright	30
WR Hammond	c Summers	b Wright	80
*BH Lyon		b Tarbox	38
FJ Seabrook		b Hill	29
+H Smith		lbw b Hill	6
WL Neale	not out		51
CJ Barnett	not out		34
EJ Stephens	did not bat		
CWL Parker	did not bat		
PT Mills	did not bat		

Extras (15 b, 9 lb, 1 nb)   25
Total (6 wickets, declared, 124 overs)   370

Fall of wickets:
1-116, 2-117, 3-225, 4-266, 5-272, 6-290

Worcestershire bowling	Overs	Mdns	Runs	Wkts
Root	37	10	82	0
Hill	20	1	71	2
Bowles	17	3	49	0
Tarbox	30	5	88	1
Wright	20	4	55	3

Worcestershire second innings

*JB Higgins	c Lyon	b Parker	35
L Wright		b Parker	1
BW Quaife	c Seabrook	b Hammond	19
WV Fox	c Lyon	b Hammond	1
HHIH Gibbons	c Lyon	b Parker	9
CF Root	lbw	b Hammond	1
CV Tarbox	c Barnett	b Hammond	29
JW King	c Seabrook	b Hammond	4
JJ Bowles	hit wkt	b Parker	20
DV Hill	st Smith	b Hammond	17
+FT Summers	not out		0
Extras (21 b, 10 lb)			31
Total (all out, 66.3 overs)			167

Fall of wickets:
1-6, 2-67, 3-69, 4-73, 5-78, 6-116, 7-117, 8-137, 9-167, 10-167 (66.3 ov)

Gloucestershire bowling	Overs	Mdns	Runs	Wkts
Hammond	33.3	5	105	6
Parker	33	22	31	4

Gloucestershire won by an innings and 168 runs

Notes:
The match was scheduled for three days but completed in two.
Hammond achieved his best innings bowling analysis in First-Class Matches in the Worcestershire first innings.

FIVE

Razors, Fags, Fowl and a Fish

'Cricket is a sport in which the basic equipment, the bat and the ball, may …
within the game's rules, quite legitimately be used as weapons.'

Anon.

Despite the best efforts of WG and family - younger brother EM was secretary for 39 years - and other great players like Walter Hammond, the Shire's trophy cupboard had remained bare for over a century.

Back in the 1990s David Graveney had raised the thorny problem. 'It's a strange thing,' he said, 'Gloucestershire can play so well in the one-day game, but really haven't played to their ability in the longer game. The four-day game is more about scoring runs, which they haven't done on a consistent basis.'

David's comment was as true today as it ever was. And bearing it in mind, I also thought again of old Bert Avery in late June 2011. Both Kevin O'Brien and Hamish Marshall, in their Gladiatorial blue, had thumped centuries as the Shire posted the highest Twenty20 total in England. Oh yes, the Middlesex bowling attack had certainly been very obliging on a friendly Uxbridge wicket.

O'Brien hit 11 sixes in his 119 off 52 deliveries as he and Marshall, 102 off 54 balls, put on 192 for the first wicket in the Shire's 254-3. That beat the 250-3 Zum made against the Shire in 2006. However, exciting stuff it may have been, Bert had always maintained the hoick and thrash game wasn't for the purist.
The very idea of it was anathema.

'I don't like the one-day cricket. I never have done,' he had confessed. 'To my mind it's just a knockabout for people. They don't play the game. They just go out there and have a swing at the ball. Okay, today everybody wants it, but I'm quite prepared to watch my own cricket club on a Saturday and Sunday, and more especially since they've got this fancy dress on. I haven't seen one yet, and I don't think I will. I just can't abide the pyjama game.'

I'd felt a bit mischievous, recalling a world where cricket sponsors seemed to manufacture nowt but razors and fags, and a bank was from where you tickled trout. 'What if Mike Proctor had played in *his* pyjamas? 'And what about '71, '73 and '77?

Bert pouted, possibly recalling the fans once going so far as to call the county 'Proctorshire'. The accolade was, surely, warranted. Between 1968 and 1981, Mike scored over 14,000 runs for the Shire, with 32 centuries, took over 800 wickets and completed over 200 catches, most of them at slip. The memory of the sunny uplands of Shire cricket blew like a zephyr breeze, momentarily parting the mists of the recent doldrums.

'We have a funny habit of getting publicity when we lose,' Bert had said. He didn't know why that should be, but he remembered the headlines the Shire got after playing in a very dimpsey Manchester surrounded by a crammed partisan crowd.

Lancashire v Gloucestershire, the Gillette Cup semi-final at Old Trafford in 1971 has become legendary – a match from a time when county cricketers made Bert less grumbly by wearing their whites in limited over affairs, and today's red 'Post Box' media centre, hinting of the one at Lord's, but a tad more half-arsed, didn't even register on the weirdest of imaginations.

With the Shire batting first, Proctor's superb 65 has almost been forgotten in the drama that followed. But it laid the foundation for a score of 229 for 6 that was more than satisfactory for the era. An hour lost to rain at lunch meant the game was concluded in, famously, ever worsening light in which, but for the crowd noise, one might have heard owls hooting.

Lancashire's Jack Simmons recalled umpire Dicky Bird panicking because of the dark. Arthur Jepson, however, was the senior umpire, and he said, 'Bugger off back behind your stumps, Dicky. We're finishing this game no matter what you say.' And Dicky did as he was told as the Shire whittled away at the Lancs batting order.

But still the Northerners edged closer to their target. They were aided and abetted by hundreds of Mancunian kids in fashionable bell-bottoms spilling onto the field, and generally getting in the way as Proctor and co. chased leather.

Maybe unwisely, the Shire continued to exhibit confidence.

Dapper John Mortimore retained a swagger, and nonchalantly put his hands in his pockets as if to express, 'there you go, easy as they come,' after he bowled Jack Simmons just as the pavilion clock ticked to 8.45. Lancs were 203 for 7. Then David Hughes strode into bat. Two overs passed with both he and Lanky-lanky-Lancashire's skipper Jack Bond being unable to pick the Shire seamers.

Mortimore did a few restrained exercises of elbows up to his chest while swiveling from the hips, and then he was in to bowl his final over. Down the wicket again came David Hughes. Within a minute no one could hold a candle to him.

'Six! A magnificent shot.' Jim Laker, one of the finest off-spinners in the history of cricket, was on BBC commentary, and audibly excited. 'A superb effort by David Hughes. It brings the scores level!'

Cue excited pitch invasion and a further brightening of the railway station lights to illuminate the last rites.

Proctor roared to the wicket and launched the ball ferociously at Jack Bond. Jack calmly clipped the much battered cherry into the off side and scampered on to be named *Wisden Cricketer of the Year*. 'There it is. That's the winning run!' Jim Laker's voice was almost drowned out by the home cheering.

When things had calmed down and celebratory pints drunk, Hughes became a tad waggish as he reflected where the boundary rope ended up after those rascally local kids, under cover of descending dark, had tugged it many a yard towards the centre. 'What you thought were big hits, I was just clearing the square with them,' he said.

Had the Shire been cheated? Still emotional many a year later, Bert would have one believe he took it on the chin. 'Oh, 'twas a fantastic match, really. One of the most astonishing one-day matches ever played. Five to nine the match finished. The lights shone from the station into the near pitch dark. It was fantastic. People missed the last train an' all.

''Yes, we were down. And we went back into the pub where we were stoppin', had a few drinks, and forgot all about it.'

Really, Bert? Pull the other one, I thought.

I raised the fateful Mortimore over with Peter West. 'I felt very sorry for John,' he reflected, rubbing a hand over his chin. 'He and fellow off spinner David Allen formed an outstanding partnership, and against Lancashire he bowled ... perfectly well. And it was one of those days when David Hughes inspired, and the ball continued to fly to all parts. John will smile about it in his old age. It can happen to anybody, but conceding 24 in that one over when Hughes launched his famous twilight assault still beggar's comprehension.'

And it was David Allen put things into perspective: 'Yes, the disappointment was tremendous. We thought we were going to win. Of course, we went onto '73, and won the Gillette Cup Final at Lord's.'

Blooming heck, the thirty-nine years since 1973 has flashed by quicker than a Tiflex ball in the backwaters of Division 2 where rugged Captain Giddo's not big on the razor.

Just recently I rediscovered a couple of grainy black and white photographs of homemade banners snapped by my Uncle Tubby during the great occasion. One had 'PROCTOR BITES YER BAILS' daubed upon it. The other was appropriate to both the sponsor and its advertising slogans of the day. It showed a white double sheet tied between two canes of bamboo declaring 'GLOSTER – A SHAVE ABOVE THE REST'.

The softly spoken David Graveney sporting a neatly pruned moustache seemed slightly bashful when describing his first year as a full-time professional cricketer. And he had found the prospect of playing in a final fairly daunting.

'I can remember sharing a room with Jimmy Foat,' he reminisced. 'We had been to school together at Millfield, and were both so excited about the match that we woke up reasonably early and got to the ground even before the gates had opened to any spectators.

'Bizarrely, we were actually refused entry. The rather conservative gateman didn't believe us that we were Gloucestershire players. What he saw in front of him were two long-haired teenagers.

'As pictures of the day will show, our hairstyles were a bit longer than they are now, and Jimmy, as a passionate supporter of Aston Villa had football stickers all over our car. The only way to satisfy the gateman that we were playing was by opening the car boot and actually getting the gear out.

'But I remember we were both standing on the Lord's balcony as young 19-year olds in a sort of empty ground with all the camera readying, and thought, this is going to be it.'

Shire skipper Tony Brown won the toss and decided to bat first. And in a total of 248 for 8 off the allotted 60 overs, only he and Mike Proctor really troubled the scorers. Proctor fell just short of a century by getting out for 94 while Brown remained not out on 77 as the innings closed. The two former Millfield lads failed to make it into double figures, but they were in good company as neither did the Shire top order of Sadiq Mohammed, Zaheer Abbas or Roger Knight.

Opening with Geoff Greenidge, the last white player to play for the West Indies, and Jeremy Morley, the Sussex reply fairly breezed along. Captain Brown took it upon himself to break the partnership by getting rid of Morley. Then both David Graveney and the bespectacled Jimmy Foat, whose hairdo made him resemble a bouffant spaniel, got themselves into the thick of things.

'Jimmy racing in from cover to run out Tony Grieg for nought was one of the turning points of the game. It nearly brought the house down.

'Sit Down You're Rocking The Foat', sang a West Country corner of Lord's.

The Aussie twang of Richie Benaud described another key moment. 'A good catch! A fine catch, there! Young Graveney coming in from point on the fence, judged it beautifully! The man out is Mike Buss, caught Graveney bowled Knight.'

Although not quite the murk of Old Trafford, the Lord's final ended in extreme gloom. Especially so for Sussex. Mike Proctor delivered the coup de gras with Jim Laker on commentary. 'Proctor steams up to the wicket. John Snow onto the back foot. Bowled him! No hope once he'd got on the back foot!'

A bunch of Shire supporters helped the English fast bowler in his trudge back to the pavilion by singing another popular song of the summer game 'I'm Just A Girl Who Can't Say Snow'.

One further run was added before Proctor shattered the stumps of Roger Marshall, the last man in.

Laker, again: 'it's all over! Proctor leaps in the air! Sussex all out for 208.

'And here come these Gloucester supporters. They've waited a very, very long time for a major victory such as this, and how they have deserved it!' To a man the Shire players ran for the pavilion ducking in ecstasy beneath the boundary rope held aloft by police and stewards as a makeshift barrier that dissuaded fans from invading the sanctum. A young Goose on the hunt for autographs even tried politely asking a police inspector to let him through. To his chagrin he was just as politely refused, and he had to watch on tip-toe among the joyous throng when Tony Brown raised the silver trophy to the heavens.

Among Tony's '73 heroes was Andy Stovold. He, though, remained modest about his contribution. 'I was the small part player, the wicketkeeper coming in to replace Roy Swetman,' he said eventually.

'What? Roy of the Bucket?' I'd exclaimed.

'Yer,' said Andy, suddenly sounding non-committal. The former boyish-looking England and Surrey 'keeper, and useful lower middle-order bat, had come out of retirement in 1972 to have three summers with the Shire. He was the chap named and shamed by Fred Titmus, for almost fuelling an international incident at the end of 1955, having become involved in a bit of 'ragging'.

In search of a jolly jape during their tour of Pakistan, a gaggle of MCC players went across to the Pakistanis' hotel. There they found Idris Begh, an umpire whose rubbish on-field decision-making had warranted fervent criticism by the tourists. To have described the bloke as 'biased' was mild, 'cheat' was probably more accurate. After plonking him in a chair, a bucket of water was tipped over his head. It's said, Roy gave the 'final shove' that resulted in Begh's soaking. By the next day, a major incident was brewing. The Pakistan manager told Begh that he had been made to look ridiculous, and the umpire appeared in front of reporters with his arm in a sling - a result, he claimed, of being manhandled by the MCC players. A telegram was sent to Lord's, and as tensions mounted, troops were quickly dispatched. The matter was diffused amidst much groveling. A diplomatic storm in a teacup, perhaps, but it wasn't good form.

Andy Stovold remained tight-lipped about any high-jinx in the Shire dressing room. Instead, he mentioned that batting number seven or eight against the likes of John Snow was 'a little bit awe-inspiring'.

'The '73 celebrations went on for about three weeks. Gloucestershire in those times if they took you in, it was a Gloucestershire win, everyone came to watch you win, bus journeys in and out of everywhere in Gloucestershire. I think, we finished up doing coach rides through Bristol. Then we went on to Wootton-under-Edge, Dursley, up through into Stroud, Cheltenham and Gloucester, and into the Forest areas, as well. I think the whole county celebrated.'

My asking David Graveney which memory of the victory tour was best made him dewy eyed. 'I always appreciated there had always been a bit of a conflict between north and south of the county,' he said. 'In fact probably our purist support came from an area were we never used to play which was the Stroud area. I can remember travelling around Stroud and the reception we had from all over the county was great, but I can remember very vividly at Stroud it was very special.' And with that he lost himself for a few moments.

David Allen still thrives on the match, calling it 'tremendous'. And he was very sure upon whom most praise should be lavished. 'The fillip Proctor gave us was that in one-day cricket was one man can dominate a lot,' he maintained. ' Sir Gary Sobers certainly did this in one-day cricket. That way you can set yourself to win four or five matches, which is one competition. It's very difficult to set yourself to win the Championship, which in those days was 28 matches. I don't think there was any doubt that Proctor set himself to win something. And the Gillette series this was one of the ways he could do it.'

Certainly, the tributes to Proctor are as numerous as leaves on a Gloucestershire apple tree. Peter West had noticed the ability of 'young Michael' very early on, first coming across him when he came over with a side from South Africa of potentially very promising young cricketers. Several of these, himself and Barry Richards included, subsequently became test cricketers.

'He played against a side I raised to play against Cranbrook, my old school in Kent', said Peter. 'And I thought then, my word, he's got a strange bowling action, but this chap can play cricket. He played a magnificent innings that day.

'And Graham Wiltshire, by then the County's cricket coach, while browsing through the School's Cricket section of *Wisden* spotted Michael's score of 148 not out he'd made against Radley College. Soon David Allen was winging a letter to Michael's parents.

'I've often thought, how much greater a batsman he would have been had not been a fast bowler taking so much out of himself. All in all he was a wonderful cricketer with a marvelous attitude to the game, and, of course, one of the overseas players who've done Gloucestershire very, very proud. And one mustn't forget he went to play for the Rest of the World when he was here, as well.'

David Graveney, too, retains a vivid impression of 'Proccy'. In the late 60s he was a houseguest of the Graveneys, and he was staying with them when the club had the unenviable decision to choose between Barry Richards and himself - indeed an embarrassment of riches. Happily, Proccy got the nod and became very close to David's family. As David said: 'He was everybody's hero.'

And I suppose, Goose's gushing praise for the great blonde South African also flowed from the soul. 'Cor,' he cooed, 'Proccy could twat 'em like billy-o.'

Thanks to Proccy it soon became clear that '73 wasn't a one off. Four years later the Shire proved it. But to be honest, man for man they were nowhere near as good a side in '77 as we were in '73.

Proccy's style of leadership, however, made up for it. He was very much one of setting the example by giving 120%, if that's possible. Every day he went out there he wore the county colours, and wanted to do well. In fact, he wanted Gloucestershire to do well, and, through his rousing play and captaincy he was inspirational to the team by his own performances

As an example take his four Hampshire wickets in five balls at Southampton in the semi-final of the Benson and Hedges Cup - Gordon Greenidge, Barry Richards, Trevor Jesty and John Rice. Just to guild the lily, David Graveney reckoned Proccy should have had a better return than a treasured hat-trick. It should have been four out of four.

'The fourth ball of that particular over bowled to Nigel Cowley was actually the plumest decision of the lot,' believed David. 'But I think because Tom Spencer the umpire had already given the hat-trick he wasn't keen to go for four in four. It nearly cost us the game because Nigel Cowley got 50, and Hampshire got reasonably close.'

Goose still enjoys a happy sigh and a smile over the affair. 'If you listen to the Gloucestershire supporters there were probably 20,000 fans there, given the number of people who say they were there for the hat-trick. It was a day to remember, as was the final when we beat Kent.'

Being 'that much older' in '77 David admitted to creating an unfortunate quandary for Proccy by the time the final arrived. The Shire had played the second round of the Gillette a few days beforehand, and David had been smashed around by Northamptonshire. As a result of this Proccy was umming and areing whether or not David ought to play.

'He decided I would be selected,' said David, 'It was a relief, but I remember being extremely nervous marking out my run and confidence not high because of Northants.

The debatable decision of David playing hadn't been a secret, however. Most notably, Richie Benaud had picked up on it, and that came across in his match commentary: 'Bowled him! The gamble has paid off!'

Bernard Julien's wicket had gone to David's second ball of the day, and suddenly his confidence was back.

The Bensons' were quite good for Andy Stovold, too. He opened the batting and kept wicket so had quite a leading role. And having won several 'Man of the Match' awards, a lot more was expected of him. Fortunately, in the '77 final, he delivered, rattling up 70 odd just after lunch before taking a phenomenal one handed leaping catch to dismiss Alan Ealham off a Martin Vernon medium pacer. And he was all very modest about it. 'I had a good game. You remember them, because you had a big part in it, really.'

In essence, the Shire also had the chance to win the Championship that year. Iron-ically they played the last game of the season against Hampshire. The side made up of a fair collection of interesting players did have the opportunities, and could have, perhaps should have, performed the double. Despite a first innings hundred from Proccy and second innings stoicism from Alastair Hignall, the Shire were scuppered in no small measure by the bats of Gordon Greenidge and, as Sod's

Law would have it, Barry Richards.

Still, according to David Allen, interviewed in the 1990s, the '70s were wonderful heady days. 'Oh dear, oh dear,' he lamented, 'we could do with one or two coming to us now.' Between 1999 and 2004 he got his wish as the world of razors was replaced by one of fags and finance, and Mark Alleyne's side suddenly emerged as the dominant force in English one-day cricket. For this achievement much credit went to Kiwi coach John Bracewell, whose arrival helped turn the Shire's under-achievers into a formidable cricket team. Most helpfully they batted all the way down in reality as well as on paper.

EM Grace was once described as 'overflowing with cricket at every pore, full of lusty life, cheerily gay, with energy inexhaustible' and some of those qualities could be seen as the Shire's winning streak began by thrashing Yorkshire by 124 runs in the Benson & Hedges Super Cup final in August 1999, with skipper Alleyne contributing 112 from just 91 balls.

Purely as a point of interest the match was the first domestic final played in front of the £5.8m singing, all dancing media centre at the Nursery End of the ground. Opened that June for Cricket World Cup, the structure resembled a spaceship hovering above the Compton and Edrich Stands. It won architectural awards. On the flip side, the huge glass frontage, offering almost 200 journalists a wonderful view of the ground, earned the nickname 'Cherie Blair's mouth'.

Then later in August came victory for Gloucestershire over Zum by 50 runs in the NatWest final. Put in to bat by Jamie Cox, the Shire effectively defended a score of 230 for eight by taking the first five Somerset wickets for 52. Jack Russell succeeded in driving more than one Somerset batsman to distraction by his antics behind the stumps. Here, one can only interpret the words of John Bracewell when he said, ' I've always believed the wicketkeeper orchestrates what goes on in the field if he is *offensive* in his attitude.'

Indeed, earlier in the match Jack had caused Andy Caddick to lose his cool by backing up too far during a valuable cameo innings that produced an unbeaten 31 and trademark extravagant leaving of the ball outside off stump.

Zum though, through Rob Turner and Keith Parsons, added 82 for their sixth wicket. Despite that partnership the last four went down for 14, and there were almost five overs left when Ian Harvey concluded the game.

Tim Hancock's aggressive 74 was the focal point of the Shire innings, although a target of 231 should have been gettable. Surely, none in the crowd could forget the anguished cry of 'NO!' from Zum skipper Jamie Cox that seemed to echo around Lord's when he was trapped ell bee by Mike Smith after only having faced four balls. By the end, three wickets each for Harvey, Alleyne and Smith made certain of a notable double. Jack Russell had four dismissals, three catches and a stump-ing. To popular acclaim, his significance with bat and gloves earned him Man of the Match.

Secretly, I'm sure on-field umpire David Shepherd, after many Gloucestershire years of his own, must have been glowing with pride.

And so began a golden era of the Shire as undisputed kings of one-day cricket bagging seven trophies in five seasons with both the C&G Trophy and the Benson & Hedges Cup being won in consecutive years.

In 2000 the B&H Cup was plain sailing, despite a magnificent 104 by Glamorgan captain Matthew Maynard in the final. Another one-day fifty by Tim Hancock gave them the necessary momentum and Matt Windows and Mark Alleyne rounded things off with 3.1 overs to spare.

Given the circumstances, BBC Bristol felt it sensible to gather some sound bites on all the excitement and so shoved a microphone towards David Graveney and asked him to comment. 'They've won so many one-day games in the past couple of years they never believe they're beaten, he said matter-of-factly, 'and when it gets down to the wire in the final overs, they just have that willpower while other people fall away.

'Three out of our four competitions are played over a shorter distance and Gloucestershire have shown themselves to be the experts at that. Their bonuses must be nearly as big as the England team's bonuses by the time they finish.'

Some folk began to question how a winning habit was achieved without the talis-man that was Mike Proctor. Well, there was an unofficial club mascot that appeared to do a damned fine job.

Enter the funky chicken sideshow. And I'm not referring to the 1970 song by the black American artist Rufus Thomas with lyrics to the effect of: 'You put both arms up across your face / Your knees start wiggling all over the place / You flap your arms / and your feet start kicking / Then you know you doin' the funky chicken.'

No, the particular funky chicken I'm talking about was real, but way beyond clucking. It would be more accurate to say it probably hummed, although this might give an erroneously musical impression for a corpse twenty-four years on the road.

Blame for the matter rests solely on a bloke from the Shire called Paul Brimble. He confessed to the BBC that a real wiggling, flapping fowl taken to Lords in 1977 didn't emerge alive. As is the habit with farm life, the bird had escaped, causing a major distraction from the cricket. And Paul had thought it best to commit foul play rather than the Shire losing concentration on the ball.

'Being young, I was quite sharp and managed to catch it and break its neck,' he said without sentiment. 'We won that cup, so from there we plucked and froze it, and took it to all the big one day games. Gloucestershire went on to rewrite the history books of one day cricket.'

Ah, but who writes the history, I thought. It's been 'put out there', probably to ward off dissent from animal rights supporters among the Shire following, that Paul didn't do the foul deed at all. What actually came to pass, the tale now goes, is that a fan mistakenly brought a frozen supermarket chicken to a game instead of his lunchbox. Really?

However, the luck of the bird gathered credence, and before long Paul was the leader of the gang of fans known as 'The Chicken Men', bringing the repeatedly refrozen fowl out for an airing and passing it around to those in crowd brave enough to handle it, and singing the anthem 'He's got the whole chicken in his hands.' And if endorsement was needed, even Mark Alleyne, when Shire captain, accorded the bird the honour of holding it aloft in trophy fashion while running the length of the Grace Pavilion at the County Ground.

For those with belief, total conviction about the bird's credentials arose in 2000. The third round of NatWest saw the Shire drawn against their local rivals Worcestershire. And it was a match that Paul and his avian companion failed to arrive at.

Worcestershire appeared to have won the tie and progressed to the quarter-finals. However, it soon came to light that in fielding teenage paceman Kabir Ali, they had made a boo-boo. He had already turned his arm over for Worcestershire's Cricket Board XI earlier in the tournament, and this was against the tournament rules.

On this, the smallest of technicalities, the Shire lodged an appeal based on Ali being an 'ineligible player'. The powers-that-be saw the Shire's point of view and decided the game should be replayed. And with both Paul and the chicken present the result was never in doubt, nor was the competition's eventual winner. As I'm sure avid Shire fans know the county went on to retain their title, marching on to beat another local rival, Warwickshire, in a rain-affected final, albeit with the assistance of Messrs Duckworth and Lewis.

Romantics suggest that the rain was merely nature's way of tearfully saying goodbye to the last NatWest. The *Telegraph* was more damning. It reported: 'The NatWest Trophy slithered out of existence last night under leaden skies when the rain that had washed away any possibility of play on Saturday returned to ruin a final that went Gloucestershire's way. Even Gloucestershire, who have now won four successive Lord's finals, will recognise that it was a sad way to say goodbye to the sponsors of domestic cricket's senior one-day competition.'

The Shire were 22 runs ahead under the Duckworth-Lewis rules for rain-affected matches when play was unable to resume before the cut-off point of 6.30pm. With the Shire declared winners the sun immediately came out to mock everybody, and people wondered why the rules were so perverse.

In truth, Mike Smith, well supported by Tim Hancock, had muzzled the Warwickshire middle order. Although, in keeping with the character of an unsatisfactory weekend, Channel 4 made an absolute horlicks of the prize-giving ceremony. And to the cricket world in general it was clear the game hadn't lived up to expectations.

On the eve the match Bracewell admitted to Scyld Berry of the *Telegraph* that the final would be 'Gloucestershire's toughest and tightest'. Both counties had plenty in common. They were the two best fielding sides in the country, with the two best county wicketkeepers; and they both batted a long way down on paper. And like the Shire had Bracewell, Warwickshire had the late Bob Woolmer as their free-thinking coach.

So, in the end, what was the defining factor between the teams? Paul Brimble was adamant the Shire's successes of 2000, like those of '99 were due, in part, to the 'mystical chicken'. Although, as far as I'm aware, he failed to mention the impact made, by the likes of Ian Harvey and Jonty Rhodes, not to mention linchpin Jack Russell.

However, given the murky debate, it's safer to say the chicken was an unofficial club mascot. And it certainly wasn't unique in being doornail dead. Alastair Hignell, an unsung member of the '77 team, happened to mention a stuffed goat - the obvious players' choice in Goatacre, a Wiltshire village on route to the national village knockout final.

As for the 'lucky' chicken, Alastair thought the palava was all down to the diet of modern-day cricketers. 'If anyone produced a chicken in my days as a player, they would have eaten it,' he said.

In 2001 Surrey fans took him at his word after Alex Tudor, Ed Giddins and Saqlain Mushtaq consigned the Shire to a heavy defeat in the B&H final. So after thirty-five matches Paul respectfully handed the thirty-five match old chicken over to the Shire's conquerors. They were a tad pissed and reportedly meandered off to gobble it. Rather them than me.

The chicken, although now a mere memory, remains in the verbiage of innuendo.

And John Light, the former County Chairman, hadn't helped matters one iota by continually mentioning that 'clutch' of titles.

But after the fortuitous fowl what next? Paul, of course, had the answer – a lucky sea bass, and he appointed himself as its keeper.

'I went fishing with the boys, and we caught a lot of sea bass,' said Paul. 'One particular fish had a lot more fight in it than the others.' After reeling the sea creature in, Paul promptly clobbered it on the noggin. Soon it was in his freezer where once had lived the 'mystical chicken'.

On match days the bass, known scientifically as Centropristis striata, was popped into a 'Mystical Container' marked with both the word 'DANGER' and with what looked misleadingly like a picture of a piranha. Most pointedly, the fish, with a dorsal fin as sharp as Excalibur, was almost becoming legendary without quite having the same kudos. Loaded aboard the 'Sea Bass Coach', fish, Paul and about forty devotees were ready for the off. They would be witness to Worcestershire becoming heartily sick of the Shire.

The Cheltenham & Gloucester Final in 2003 fittingly saw Gloucestershire beat them by 7 wickets. Ian Harvey got 'Man of the Match'. Before going on to wallop 61 in a knock that included twelve fours he nabbed the top order wickets of Anurag Singh and Graeme Hick, the latter making a quacker. And all this from an originally underrated all-rounder hailing from the Australian backwater of Wonthaggi.

Signed by the Shire on the cusp of their glorious era in early 1999, Ian arrived to replace Courtney Walsh as the county's overseas player, in a move the media called 'shrewd'. The club had made its mind up about him on the say so of the Aussie Test batsman Allan Border. I mean, the guy had credentials - a season with Shire and a game or two for Downend. The grizzled wonder guaranteed that both Ian's positive outlook and high level of ability would be 'desirable attributes'.

And how right he was. Time would prove the decision to be a masterstroke as the unassuming Ian not only became a proper talisman on a par with Proccy, but also began to transform the attitudes of his teammates, just as John Bracewell had wanted his overseas player to do. David Foot, seldom prone to hyperbole, concluded: 'Few imports have ever been so influential.'

Few batsmen have the capacity to incite the same level of excitement that proceeded Ian Harvey's stroll to the wicket whenever he was representing his beloved Shire. Whatever the situation, whoever the rivals, the crowds whether at Nevil Road, Gloucester or Cheltenham knew Harvey's response was only going to be a belligerent counterattack. His extensive array of shots all around the wicket left bowlers utterly deflated. Held up his bowling sleeve was one of the wickedest slower balls in the business. This, mixed up with unsloggable low-rjectory yorkers, shock bumpers, and skidding bounce, made him a whole bundle of trouble for the opposition.

Today, in the reign of Captain Giddo Ian's a fellow still held close to the hearts of Shire fans. They tend to stand beneath the Sky Sports commentary box when Ian is seen sitting in a pundit's chair, and shout up: 'Bring back Harvey! Bring back Harvey!' It must feel nice to be so appreciated. Worcestershire, though, might defer on that point.

In 2004, and again in the C&G competition, the margin of defeat for Worcestershire by 8 wickets was a tad worse than the year before. This time, around, despite a stoic ton from Vikram Solanki, Phil Weston and Craig Spearman did a winning job with the bat.

Oh, how the blooming bass was waved! But by the end of the 2004 season both the fish and Paul appear to have vanished in the same manner as Shire success.

Yet, stranger than the disappearance of any dubious Shire mascot, was the trend-setting absence of cash in the coffers. The whingers in accounts departments complained the county lost money on the series of one-day finals wins - ironic given the entry of the financial world into cricket sponsorship. However, I suppose such losses might, in some way, be put down to the cost of razors and fags, and the wide berth given to the wafted niffs from rotting fowl and fish.

The Golden Years of One-Day Cricket

Benson & Hedges Super Cup 1999
Gloucestershire v Yorkshire
Gloucestershire won by 124 runs

Note: The B&H competition in 1999 was an eight-team affair, with those finishing in the top eight of 1998's County Championship qualifying.

NatWest Bank Trophy 1999
Gloucestershire v Somerset
Gloucestershire won by 50 runs.

Benson & Hedges Cup 2000
Gloucestershire v Glamorgan
Gloucestershire won by 7 wickets.

NatWest Bank Trophy 2000
Gloucestershire v Warwickshire
Gloucestershire beat Warwickshire by 22 runs (D/L method).

NatWest Bank Trophy 2003
Gloucestershire v Worcestershire
Gloucestershire won by 7 wickets.

NatWest Bank Trophy 2004
Gloucestershire v Worcestershire
Gloucestershire won by 8 wickets.

Brewing Uncertainty

'While there is tea, there is hope.'
Sir Arthur Wing Pinero

Jeremy Paxman was very clear - the English love their tea. And, through the trade of Indian opium, Britain created 12 million drug addicts in China to get it, which was reprehensible to say the least. But to allow the odd cricketer the enjoyment of a cuppa, some might say, any sacrifice was in the best possible taste.

As it turned out, Bomber Wells who had, in the words of Michael Parkinson, 'a summer's day in his face and laughter in his soul', liked his brew served in only the best china.

Everyone likes a good story and Bomber Wells, during a life innings that, sadly, ended in 2008, could tell one or two. Certainly, his involvement in mix-ups running between the wickets were as common as pints of Gloucestershire cider.

'For God's sake, call,' Sam Cook once begged him.

'Heads!' came back Bomber's reply. It was an apt call as his nickname was a reference to the former British heavyweight boxer 'Bombardier' Billy Wells who struck the gong at the start of films made by the Rank studios.

Happily, he never changed his character from the carefree club cricketer he'd been when first summoned to play for the county. Bomber was sat in Gloucester Park tucking into fish and chips with his girlfriend when the call had come, delivered by the giant of a man that was Tom Goddard. The gurt chap had crocked himself and the Shire needed a bowler.

Some things Bomber claimed, however, had to be taken with a pinch of salt. For instance, him bowling the fastest over in cricket during the time it took for the bells of Worcester Cathedral to strike noon, which is approximately thirty-four seconds. Likely tales such as this, as with many of his after dinner stories, were included in his book '*Well, Well, Wells!*' published in 1982.

A couple immediately spring to mind. Before Bomber's very first match for the Shire he had to borrow kit in order to play, and travelled to the game by bus. Also he was renowned for a distaste of physical exercise, and so developed a run-up of just one or two paces. Batsmen, he claimed, found it hard to adjust to this unusual style. 'I took five wickets in my first match. And I know at least two of them weren't looking,' he would cheerfully tell audiences.

His off-breaks took 998 wickets in first class cricket. And he famously declined the opportunity to play in the last game of his final first class season in 1965. He was under the misapprehension he had 999 wickets. 'Lots of people have taken 1000 wickets, he told the Nottinghamshire skipper Geoff Millman. 'Nobody has taken 999.' Oh fiddlesticks, Bomber, the memory, the memory.

And on this note, being blessed with the opportunity of interviewing him myself, I came across a particular favourite anecdote of mine while shuffling through the recordings.

'It was a hot Tuesday afternoon.' said Bomber, 'We were playing Somerset on our sand heap. And we done them easy in the first innings. But now in the second innings there was no sand on it. They were uncovered wickets, you see, and the wind had got up in the night and actually blew the sand off. Well you couldn't sweep it back on, so it was a different type of pitch. And we were trying to get the Somerset skipper Gerry Tordoff out, and Cooky and myself toiled away without success. And I was deposited on the mid wicket boundary out of the way, and the ball never came to me.

'And I was standing there and an old dear, about twenty yards away, said, "Do you want a drink, Bomb?"

'And I said, "Oh, yes please."

"It's a cup of tea. That's all I've got."

'I said, "That's all right." And in the course of two overs I moved gradually from mid wicket down into cow corner, down towards long on somewhere. And I was having this cup of tea when Cooky, for once in his life, bowled a bad ball. He bowled this full toss. And old Gerry hit it. Course shouldn't have been no one down in that area, see.

'So I was there drinking this cup of tea, and I watched this ball and thought, that's going straight down my throat. And it did! And this old dear, she was looking at this ball. Fact is *no one* was looking. And I couldn't hand my cup of tea to *anyone*. So I just stood there with a cup of tea in one hand, and hoped to God I'd catch this ball one-handed with the other one. And then I did!

'Marvelous. Great. Threw it in. Carried on drinking my cup of tea. And we went on to win the match unfortunately for them, fortunately for us. Afterwards Emmett, who was a tyrant, but a great, great, great captain, came in the dressing room and said, "Bomber, you're not playing in the next two matches."

'I said, "Why?"

"Because I put you at mid wicket."

"Ah, but if I had been at mid wicket I wouldn't of caught him out."

"Makes no difference. When you're put at mid wicket, you stay there."'

There's an old adage held to by a journalist acquaintance of mine of 'never let the truth spoil a good story'. Much for my own conscience, I'm not a journalist but do enjoy looking things up, especially when surrounded on a daily basis by neighbours from Zum.

Gerry Tordoff, due to his commitment to the Royal Navy, only captained Somerset for one season, and that was in 1955. His short tenure wasn't a success, Zum ending up with the County Championship's wooden spoon for the fourth consecutive season. *Wisden* commented: 'From the beginning Tordoff found his batting order a jig-saw puzzle without the right men to fit the holes.' When Zum played the Shire at Nevil Road he was out second innings caught Rochford, bowled Lambert for 4. Also, the match was drawn.

I delved into the archives. Nowhere in the 1950s era of George Emmett captaining the Shire at Bristol could I find a batsman falling 'caught Wells bowled Cook', apart from on one occasion. This was John Warr of Middlesex, and he was to become that county's captain in 1958. And Middlesex did lose to the Shire at Nevil Road in 1955 on a weather-affected pitch.

But to have Bomber taking a catch against Zum whilst holding a cup of tea is so much more the romantic image of West Country cricket given that a Zum player once went out to bat still licking at an ice cream cone.

SEVEN

Raised Digits, Cupcakes and Questions

'Each well-known feature we espy:
The turf so grateful to the eye,
The Players dressed in flannels white,
And Umpires hailed with great delight.'

Anon.

It's uncertain exactly when Pucklechurch Cricket Club was formed. Locals that cite a dramatic match between Pucklechurch and Shakespeare that 'resulted in a victory for the home team by an innings and 17 runs to spare' only serves to befuddle matters. So it's best to plump for somewhere around 1878. The *Bristol Mercury & Daily Post* mentions a game in the May of that year when Pucklechurch failed to chase down a Clifton Alliance score of 71, falling well short by 28 runs.

Since then, the huge sloping field called the 'Burrell', once owned by a Bristol brewery, has been sold off and partitioned up. Today, at the bottom end is the new village cricket pitch, where metal framed canvas sightscreens billow like sails in the winds, and the tidy, solid pavilion, and a wooden groundsman's shed, are overlooked by a hugger-mugger of council housing.

Yet, 'quaint' Pucklechurch, with its fine views east towards the Cotswolds, has an interesting history. Here in 946, according to Higden's *Polychronicon*, King Edmund was cut into 'smalle partes by men longyng to the kynge'. Much later an RAF base arrived only to be transferred to the HM Prison Service to become a Young Offenders institution. And, with Parkfield Colliery down the road now closed, some still get confused between the whereabouts of minors and miners.

But what had tickled my curiosity to the extent of feeling compelled to visit the village? It was a rhetorical question. The answer, quite honestly, had been a pair of trousers. I mean, what could possibly have possessed anyone to award a club member a pair of trousers for his excellent bowling average? The mind boggles, yet the 1893 *Parish Magazine* didn't elucidate. So I felt the need to ask somebody who might know. Before I could do so I got waylaid by the cricket tea.

Gail and Lewis, assisted by Sarah, were in competition for cupcake of the week. 'Mr Whippy' played 'White Chocolate and Strawberry' and opinion as to the tastiest seemed equally divided. A plethora of hands reached out for crumbs to satisfy the judgment of individual tastes.

It had me thinking of North Nibley, a Cotswold place of manicured hedges and nails, where a rota system of proud ladies taking turns in tea creation has led to fierce feuding that would faze even the most ardent Pucklechurch cupcaker.

Apt, I suppose, as Nibley has the striking fact of being the last battle fought in England wholly between the private armies of feudal fat cats. Today, smoked salmon will vie with previous week's scones and cream, homemade cakes, or kebabs, laid out in a notable place of quintessential Englishness. For in the shadow of Breakheart Hill, tea is 'taken' inside the billiard room of Nibley House, which, with more wings than a pair of sparrows, is the Georgian country pile of the Eley family. No spikes allowed, of course.

As they fill their faces, players are careful with their crumbs, and mind their Ps and Qs. They also hold in their belches until they bend to do up their bootlaces once more, if ears didn't deceive. Manners are important.

Tea, though, was the home side's secret weapon in the Pratt Cup, as Pratt rules dictate the visitors bat first. Reputation, however, can come as a warning. And I was witness to Hillesley CC, and not North Nibley, nibbling. Digestive restraint can be a winning virtue, as admirable as any shown outside the off stump.

Even so, a modest defeat by 9 runs, I thought, could have been averted had the home batters been less reluctant to take those quick singles on their pretty field. Indeed, it was runner up in the *Daily Telegraph's* 'Willow Walks' competition 2008 to find Britain's Best Village Cricket Ground. It lost out to Bridgetown CC in Zum that benefits from an endearing thatched wooden pavilion.

Although comfortably taking the title for Gloucestershire would North Nibley have fared any different if it, too, had a pavilion, instead of having one of 'some nature'? Well, that was the £100,000 question. And now the whole village was raising the dosh as best it could, leaving no stone unturned. A building of substance had been decided upon. One of concrete and tile rather than thatch and slat to accommodate not only the cricket club, but also the Nibley Nobblers footballers, and school sports.

The fact is, for the thirty-odd years of the club's existence the cricket club has made do with a boundary edge gazebo. The flappy canvas and flimsy framed structure, now a bit the worse for wear, has been struggled together before the start of each game. Andy Kinnear, the chap delegated to being Club Press Officer was a bit tongue in cheek about players making do with such Spartan changing facilities.

'Most players turn up in their kit,' he said. 'Then after the match we go back to the pub all sweaty, or get changed on the grass and try and preserve our modesty as best we can.

'But we have tea in next-door Nibley House. It's a completely sublime and ridiculous situation.'

Never has a truer word been spoken in jest.

'I'm just proper glad there's no ginger cake amongst this spread had Dave bin 'ere,' said a buxom woman of middling years, lurching my mind back to Pucklechurch.

Something compelled me to ask why that was.

'They'd be nuffin left fer Dave ta use as antipersperwhatzit.'

It turned out that Dave, who used to raise a digit or two in the Gloucestershire County Cricket League, had been the bane of the cricket tea ladies before he emigrated to the east coast of Australia. Although not one for totally stuffing his fizzog, his habit on hot afternoons was to rub a bit of ginger cake under his arm as antiperspirant.

Umpires, even the professional ones, I reflected, can beings of strange habit.

Losing myself to abstraction, I thought of Dickie Bird. Not to be confused with Barnsley Beeches where Mrs Hart was a tea lady for over fifty years, Dickie, on the face of it, was a conservative chap from the land of Barnsley chops. However, 'Freethy', a bit of a clever-clogs, had put the kibosh on that notion. 'At a Cambridge Uni match at Fenners,' he informed, 'we once added a tasty marmite-chutney-cheese filling into the middle of a large jam doughnut and presented it to the venerable Dickie at tea. He gobbled it up as if nothing amiss.'

And this the man who was supposed to be taken extremely seriously when, together with Barry Meyer, he first tried the Weston photometers, created by boffin Patrick Eager, used to test the light during the Lord's Test against New Zealand in 1978.

Of course, Barry was the bloke, some say, though lacking foodie foibles, who courted controversy. How he managed to draw international attention on one occasion was seen as ironic. As well as having been one of the great former Shire wicketkeepers, he was not first umpire to apologise to a batsman for a goof. But the one he made during the 1984 Lord's Test between England and the West Indies was definitely a goody.

Barry declared a rampaging Viv Richards out ell bee to a 'nut' that would probably have missed not only the leg stump, but endangered the square-leg umpire. Perhaps, though, I exaggerate the delivery a tad. Happily, Barry eventually saw the light, and later in the evening did the right thing. He apologised to Viv, who in turn shrugged the incident off. It was Barry's apology rather than his original decision that made big media news.

And when it came to judgment on honest mistakes Jack Crapp was questionable. His first breath was taken in St Columb Major in Cornwall, England's 'crooked leg'. However, he began his career not far from Pucklechurch at Stapleton Cricket Club, scoring a quacker for the third team on his debut. Despite this, Wally Hammond's gimlet eye somehow saw Jack's potential and many seasons of representative Shire cricket and captaincy followed.

On retirement as a player in 1956 Jack went on to become an umpire for twenty-two seasons. This included standing in four Test matches, most notably the match in which Fred Trueman took his 300th Test wicket. For years and years, Fred proudly showed people the ball he used to take the wicket with. But all was not as it had seemed. Shortly before his demise, Jack owned up to journalist, Frank Keating, that he had swapped the cherries, denying Fred the historic ball. One can only hope Jack's kleptomania hadn't denied himself the open gates of St. Peter.

However, there's no doubting umpires can get away with blue bloody murder from the moment he pronounces 'Play'. Fact. Rule number one is that to undermine the white-coated one's authority just isn't cricket. If an umpire felt compelled to quote from Shakespeare takes bets on that line from *The Tempest* 'No tongue: all eyes: be silent.' Back in the good old days Richie Benaud was prone to the occasional harrumph followed by 'I'll leave you to make your own minds up about that one'.

With an umpire's life being so iffy, euphemism will have its day when bluntness could otherwise lead to blows. Being 'given out' for example, is a gift-wrapped decision deserving of thank-you letters from the fielding side. The integrity of genuine mistake can be tempered by pity, by panic or by those guesstimates after having been otherwise distracted. One is reluctant to add to this list psychological bullying - in which case the umpire must weigh up, without too much hesitation, whom he will least upset as post game post mortems at the bar can prove problematic dissections should he not have 2-litre turbo for a quick getaway.

None of this was ever a headache to the comfortably built chap out pottering his dog I happened to cross paths with in Instow, one of those North Devon coastal places you really have to *want* to go to on a chilly November day.

He acknowledged me with a friendly 'Mornin'.

'And a good morning to you, Sir,' I replied, little realising he was a hero battling vainly against lung cancer. It was 2008, and I'd passed him by in a world of my own, absorbed in researching the writer Rudyard Kipling and his semi-autobiographical book *Stalky and Co.* about the pranks and adventures of three Westward Ho! schoolboys.

Both the book and the area held certain nostalgia for me. Bideford, down the road a bit, was where I'd spent bullied school days going AWOL from Maths and Science, preferring instead to sit on rocks by the sea and attract the Headmaster's letters home. Now, those buildings of academia, so reluctantly frequented, are boarded up and wire fenced off. And the sports pitches where I'd received heavy bruising at silly point, and failed miserably in attempts to tonk balls into the Abbotsham Road, had become an idyll of thistles, enough to give Eeyore an orgasm.

Gawd, I thought, suddenly stopping in my tracks, the chap with the pooch was from 'Biddy', too - a long hike from where the globe had once known him. In a former life, as I gazed at sea spume, he'd cracked a ball so hard into the Gloucestershire crowd that it knocked out a spectator daft enough to be reading a newspaper. Taken to A&E the unfortunate recovered with little other than hurt pride.

The perpetrator with the ruddy face of a countryman had a forte for fine shot placement, and one had to admit an open broadsheet was an inviting target. Conversely, he had little talent as a bowler taking only one more first-class wicket than Jack Russell, namely two, in his entire Shire playing career that stretched from 1965 to 1979.

Then one day David Shepherd MBE discovered the joys of umpiring, a craft that would make him famous and become a beloved role model. The discipline was in his blood. His postmaster dad Herbert was also an umpire.

Shep's second life in cricket began officially in 1981 when he was appointed as a first-class umpire and handed that large white coat. By 1985 he was standing in his first Test, the fourth Test of the Ashes series at Old Trafford. Stood with him was Dickie Bird. From that moment on Shep became the rotund fixture of fairness and competence of three successive World Cup finals -1996, 1999, and 2003 - and six tournaments overall.

Ask anyone old enough to remember Shep's most famous quirk and the reply is always the same - his hopping habit. Whenever the score reached 'Nelson', that's to say 111, in a ritual dating back to his childhood cricket team days, he'd lift one foot off the ground. The number and it's multiples are considered unlucky for the batsman by folk of superstitious persuasion, and Shep's West Country neck of the woods was abundant with goblins and fairies. So, should the score tick onto 222 or 333, the crowd would wait expectant for Shep to be hopping again.

Another trademark was his tendency to undulate his hand in a sweep from left to right while signalling fours. Even today, his action has embedded itself in the public psyche with many a cricket fan becoming a mimic in celebrating a boundary.

He naturally had his disappointments, such as when he missed three wicket-taking no-balls as Pakistan surged back to beat England in the final session at Old Trafford in 2001. The journalist David Frith noted Shep came close to quitting after those fateful errors, but friends reasoned with him and he went on to serve international cricket impressively for a further four years.

'He was an umpire completely free of pomposity and malice,' wrote Frith, 'whose mistakes could therefore so easily be forgiven.'

As his retirement loomed, Shep was cherished wherever he went. During the series between New Zealand and Australia in March 2005 he was given a guard of honour by both teams.

Come early June and the second Test between West Indies and Pakistan at Kingston, Jamaica finally marked the end of Shep's career as a Test umpire. Before the game began the journo Nagraj Gollapudi got reactions on the cherished devonian from players who often nattered to him on and off the field. Zaheer Abbas didn't disappoint.

'During my early days at Gloucester,' he said, 'I used to think what kind of a player Shepherd would be considering his weight and body size. But I realised that the amount of runs he had scored was remarkable. He was a fighter and scored when Gloucestershire needed him to. He enjoyed his life and kept everyone happy. I always enjoyed having him at the other end, but whenever I was batting on 111 he would be lifting one of his legs, and I would shout, "What (are) you doing, man. Can't you stand still?" And he would say, "No, I can't."

'And he carried that hopping tradition to his umpiring job. His record clearly showed that not only was he an able player but a successful umpire too. Never a guy to get disturbed easily, Shepherd was an immaculate character - he would always be dressed elegantly with his tie and blazer at hand before and after the game.'

Zed's was just one of the voices that spoke to Gollapudi. If I had to choose a poignant tribute to Shep I'd go for the one provided by Zimbabwe captain

Tatenda Taibu as it also illustrates the true nature of cricket sportsmanship. 'The first thing that comes to mind,' he recalled, 'is the game against India when I bat-padded a delivery from Bhajji (Harbhajan Singh) to short leg and walked. After the day's play Shepherd came to me and said, "Well walked young man, I hadn't seen the edge, thank you." Since then I have been full of respect for him because if a man of his stature can find time to thank a young boy who is only playing his third Test, it's just heart warming.'

Oh yes, Shep thrived on fair play. There are those who still raise eyebrows as they recall him clapping like a circus seal when the Aussie keeper Ian Healy had the honesty to admit a 'catch' hadn't carried.

At the conclusion of the Jamaica Test, a 136-run win to Pakistan, the Windies skipper Brian Lara presented Shep with a bat inscribed: 'Thank you for the service, the memories and the professionalism. Enjoy your retirement.'

He was, in fact, given special dispensation by the ICC to umpire in an England Test at Lords as his final Test, but typical of Shep he turned the opportunity down to maintain the ICC's neutral umpiring policy for Test matches. And to date, only Steve Bucknor and Rudi Koertzen have stood in more Tests.

Fittingly, his final county appearance came at Bristol.

Sadly, within twelve months of our brief exchange of pleasantries at Instow, Shep was dead. He was 68, and had been helping his elder brother Bill run a village paper shop. His *Wisden* obituary read: 'the authorities struggle for a definition of the Spirit of Cricket. Perhaps the best answer is David Shepherd.' His fellow umpire Simon Taufel added, 'the players had this enormous respect for him as a person. He put them at their ease and forged relationships that crossed all cultural and political divides.'

In a nutshell David Shepherd was the very epitome of the English sportsman, and those who remember him would serve cricket well if they recalled at every opportunity how he always kept things in proper proportion. And he smiled a lot.

With the villagers of Pucklechurch having taken the field for the post tea session I noticed one the umpires out in the middle had three sun hats and two sets of sunglasses on his head, and his ample waist was further plumped out by having three sweaters tied around it. A Shep in the making, I thought. Then again, many a Shire village tea scoffer had the middling wobbles.

For my part I'd got so distracted I quite forgot to ask about the historic award of a pair of trousers. And what had won best cupcake escaped me. Although, if my fingers didn't lie, it was 'White Chocolate and Strawberry'.

Middling Wobbles

EIGHT

New-Fangled Cuts and Clip-Clops

'The sky is blue so we know where to stop mowing.'
Reinhold Weege, writer.

Prone to mowing, perfecting a square cut proved difficult to Goose. He blamed molehills, and declared 'Chippin' Sodbury' swear words. I bore this mind when, as we wittered on about trivial stuff, Goose raised the topic of bowling technique. This, we agreed, was something that artists admirably caught on canvas before the age of photography.

And some artist or other had oil painted a cricket scene depicting an underarm bowler amusing a smattering of genteel spectators in top hats and tails. The picture was called *'Gloucester v Somerset 1831'*. Boffins are adamant that the match is really between Cliftonians and Lansdown, and they cite the setting as being the Duke of Beaufort's country pile, Badminton House. Which to the uninitiated is very near to Chipping Sodbury.

Recently, Goose had come across a fusty print of the picture. He passed it to me. The detail warranted the focus of both our attentions.

'Dangerous stuff underarm bowlin', ' Goose said. 'D'ya think the bloke's trying to kill a fox? We're talking about the bleedin' Beauforts' here, after all.'

'Never a truer word spoken in jest my dear ol'chapper. Remember Brown's dog?'

'Oh bugger, yes.'

History tells us that forcefully underarming a cricket ball can have consequences.

This was no better shown than by George Brown while playing for Hampshire eleven years before the Badminton artist picked up his palette and brushes.

A man who could throw a ball a record 137 yards, George was noted for the terrific speed of his underarm bowling. Indeed, it was so fast that it was not always safe to bowl him. A spectator once tried to stop the ball with his coat, but George 'bowled right through it' and an unfortunate dog snoozing on the other side was bumped off; as dead as the proverbial parrot.

'Were they playing on a sward, paddock or field?'

'Lord's,' I said.

'Ah.' Goose understood immediately.

The length of grass was surely a factor in fate. The dog could have survived had the grass been longer, the ball holding up. Especially if dew was around. The ball wouldn't have skidded on as much. But with the grass kept really short, well, oops.

I pointed at the artist's impression of the Duke's level playing field. 'How d'you think His Grace tended his acreage?'

By name alone, Goose proved worthy of an opinion. 'Geese,' he said. 'Geese are great at the keeping the grass down. They're a mite partial to buttercups, celandines and daisies; and much more thorough than cows, or ponies. Scythes are just bloody hard work. Then again Thornbury's outfield was manicured by a flock of sheep. I think sheep for the outfield and ... shears for the wicket.'

'Possible, possible,' I said, thinking of my daughter having no alternative other than to cut her garden grass with a blunt pair of kitchen scissors. But how would she have coped at the likes of Thornbury, when, during the First World War, the field was used for hay making. Then came a flash of inspiration. 'Suppose the Badminton crowd used a Budding?'

I thought this a fair question. Moneyed types often procured the new-fangled in order to impress. And one such localized fanglement changed the face of cricket in the Shire, and the world beyond, forever. I speculated the Duke might have made an 'investment', the result attracting the artist's eye. For in the Year of the Dead Dog, 1830, Edwin Beard Budding, an engineer whose very name suggested a leaning towards rural stubble, invented the mowing machine.

His early machines were all made out of cast iron at the Phoenix Foundry within Stroud's Thrupp Mill, and featured a large rear roller with a cutting cylinder in the front. Cast iron gear wheels transmitted power from the rear roller to the cutting cylinder. Basically, Budding's wizardry was remarkably similar to mowers that delight the caring groundsmen of today.

As I rambled on about Budding's legacy, Goose was smiling, clearly pondering on something completely different. 'Mentioning Thornbury has got me thinkin'. Wasn't W G. Grace involved with Thornbury?'

'So I've been told, as were his brothers E.M. and Fred,' I said, not sure were this was leading. 'And?'

'Well, there's a connection between W.G., *His* Grace, and the picture.'

Bless him, Goose was right.

When W.G. celebrated his 100th hundred with champagne, few could have prophesized what the connection would be. But, in 1948, as the Shire played Derbyshire, the Gloucestershire President, the 10th Duke of Beaufort marked the centenary of W.G's birth by unveiling the memorial plaque on the Shire's Nevil Road gates. Poignantly, the Beaufort title referred to a castle in Champagne. Not meaning a celebratory drowning in the stuff, but rather the commune, now called Montmorency-Beaufort, this offered a peremptory note of warning. Cricket wasn't at the top of the French agenda. And, so it proved.

A year later, the 10th Duke surprised many Shire cricket lovers with the appearance of Golden Willow at his home. Some could be forgiven in thinking this a good thing, perhaps heralding a collection of notable souvenir cricket bats, used by the likes of Dipper, Hammond, Jessop, or even the great WG. They were foolishly mistaken.

Golden Willow was a clip-clop - the first winner out of 22 starters of the first Badminton Horse Trials. The event, dreamed up by the Duke, put the kibosh on the old cricket pitch prettily portrayed in Goose's rural scene.

Now hooves gouge clods from a turf where men once panted after leather. Underarm deeds are long forgotten. It's the genteel dressage and show-jumping arenas that absorb the attentions of the nobs and their dogs.

'Oh, Chippin' Sodbury,' concluded Goose, putting away the cricket picture. He was most accurate in saying ponies keep the grass down, even if they aren't the most thorough at it.

Spell Check and Warnings

*'Forward, forward let us range, Let the great world spin
for ever down the ringing grooves of change.'*
Alfred, Lord Tennyson (English poet, 1809-1892).

It was the stuff about which Gladiators were made. The Romans, bless them, had invited themselves to Cirencester, and forgot a pot of coins a tad further back down the Londinium Road in a little place that became Ampney Crucis.

After a friendly tip-off, I followed custom, and invited myself to Ampney Crucis after it had entered 'Gloucestershire Vibrant', an opportunity for Cotswold communities to showcase themselves.

Apart from the pétanque court, the village is the normal sort of English affair - a parish church, and a cricket pitch boasting a smart pavilion, a pub behind the wicket, the odd player, like the Honorary Fixture Secretary, coveting a linseeded bat, and tall poplar trees standing to leg, casting long shadows.

The gossip reaching my ear was the local celebrity cum organic farmer had a new celebrity partner. And the couple, had not only made it on to Elton John's 'White Tie and Tiara Ball' guest list, they were causing much ado in Ampney Crucis, too.

About to pay a much-heralded visit, their timing wasn't exactly great. On the eve of the village summer fête, a problem lay pitch-side of the little footbridge behind the *Crown of Crucis*, wherein a small band of chunterers gathered. And, as is often the way with local politics, no one was actually pointing a finger.

However, although it was perhaps my imagination, the rhubarb-rhubarb pub chatter suddenly hushed.

'It's bloody crime,' said a studious chap in spectacles, deserving raised eyebrows from the liberal minded. The laws were very strict, hereabouts. Take for example the case of local lass Mary Ann Hodge that occurred forty years, give or take, before the cricket club was founded in 1869. She stole two dresses from her employer. Appearing before the local squire and a Doctor of Divinity, Mary Ann was found guilty and sentenced to death. Although this was later commuted to deportation for life, it seemed a bit harsh.

Unsurprising then, that in June 2011, locals had nervously tapped into their PC spell-checks or reached for dusty dictionaries.

'They'll think we're a bunch of illiterates,' was the opinion of a red-faced tweed-jacketed soul of well-matured years.

'Well, how come nobody noticed it?' commented a Fat Face sweatshirt - a remark that went down like a lead balloon.

There was one certainty. No time remained to amend matters before the arrival of the two VIPs, or before the paparazzi sold photos that would make the discovered signage 'misprint' go global.

'For God's sake, *she's* going to cut the ribbon right underneath it.'

'Supposing we ask nicely. Perhaps the photographers will crop their images.'

'But what will *she* think? And more important, what will *he* think? He's a bloody cricketer.'

'He's an Australian cricketer. He probably won't notice.'

'You patronizing bastard. Stop casting aspersions.'

'They're casting *him* in bronze. And intend to plonk him in Melbourne's Yara Park.'

A cultured voice felt things were leaving the point. 'You *can* spell it the way we have. It's not totally wrong. It's just flaming obsolete.'

Perhaps clutching at straws, an arty-fart pleaded mitigation: 'Agreed, but it isn't obsolete in the names of theatres. And, that cricket pitch out the back is our very own theatre of dreams.'

'Hardly. Can't we just take the bloody sign down?'

'NO!'

Then a lady in a purple shawl said something sensible. 'It's not about spelling. Nor is it about Liz Hurley and Shane Warne. It's about Dick. And that sign's got Dick's name on it.'

That shut everyone up. Dick with his bushy white sideburns and flat cap was part of the local scenery, especially when driving his old tractor on summer missions, mowing the cricket field.

Folk foreign to the Shire may recognise the name 'Ampney Crucis' as belonging to a comic book character - a dashing, smart and charming young lord with slicked back Brylcreemed hair, monocle, and a penchant for strawberry ice cream. Created by Ian Edginton and Simon Davis, he had the ability to sense the presence of entities that exist beyond our reality in 1920s England.

To long-time friends like John Light, the former Chairman of Gloucestershire CCC who'd stepped down in 2009, Dick was 'Mister Ampney Crucis'. The title proved a fitting epitaph.

Unfortunately, a voluntary contributor had jumped the gun a bit in the August/ September 2010 issue of the *Ampney Times* when he wrote: '90 Years old on 4th September. Dick Gearing, the son of the local baker, was born and bred in Ampney Crucis ... he has been an avid sportsman, playing cricket and football from a very young age for the village team ... today he is still President and Groundsman of the cricket club. Very many congratulations and well done Dick.'

Dick never saw that birthday. He had died in the early part of August. The hole that he left in that corner of the Shire was immense. So much so that John Light thought it fitting that he himself should pay personal tribute.

Like Dick, John, too, was of the Cotswolds. A chap in his late 60s, he'd learned his early cricket on the Laurie Lee Field encircled by the gurt beeches of Sheepscombe Hill.

Indeed, his Great Aunt Annie was Laurie Lee's mum, and he well remembers his first meeting with Laurie: 'I'm three or four and I hear a strange noise downstairs. I creep and sit on the stairs, wrapped in a blanket, and there is this noise, like something I've never heard. So I have to open the door. And there's Laurie, playing his violin.'

As a whippersnapper, John was described by the current Master of the Queen's Music, as 'a slow Cotswold farm child,' and a 'terrible task' to teach. But that was at a time when the said Master was a Cirencester grammar school teacher.

By going to university John put paid to such misplaced notions.

Yet, the somewhat disparaging remarks were in the same vein as that made by John's dad, a Cotswold forester and the first post-war captain of Sheepscombe Cricket Club. He said 'a working class Cotswold lad has more chance of passing through the eye of a needle than getting onto *that* committee.'

Over the years he and Dick had frequently rubbed shoulders whilst playing on opposing village teams, and afterwards in the bar. They were kindred spirits.

'The love Dick had for his village shone through whatever he did,' wrote John. 'He was still playing for Ampney Crucis CC at the age of 65 … and when he retired he did his utmost to keep games going in the village. He was the first chairman of the Cotswold and District Cricket Association and with Williamstrip, Bibury and Bradleys, he led Ampney into the first Cirencester League.

'Always good value on the field, and more so in the pub after, Dick made many friends in the game. Finding players was no problem at all. People were coming considerable distances to play.

'A keen gardener, Dick's plant stall at Ampney fete was legendary. It is rumoured that umpires and referees were grateful recipients to surplus garden produce.

To live in a vibrant Cotswold village is a privilege. Dick Gearing did so much to make Ampney Crucis exactly that.'

Unsurprisingly, the villagers, too, wanted to make their own tribute. They did so by naming the cricket pavilion in his memory. Or as the sign above the pavilion door read: 'The Dick Gearing Pavillion'. Hellfire, that was one too many ells.

The fêted day dawned to offer anorak weather, stalls arrayed on the cricket field, and a gossip writer from the *Daily Mail*, keenly awaiting the arrival of Liz, she of the famous safety-pin dress, and her famous leg spinning beau.

Liz's long term ex Hugh Grant hadn't minced words in his belief that cricket is an aphrodisiac. 'Women do love a cricketer,' he's recorded as having said. 'It's one of those things. It's like Aston Martins. They just love it. I think they like the whites. They like the bit of red from the ball that's rubbed off on the groin area.'

And as the cricket fans anywhere could confirm Shane Warne, no longer 'on fire' but still smoking, did a lot of rubbing. And, although a candidate for hair-restorer, it's doubtful the 'Wizard of Oz' followed Jacques Kallis' anti-balding advice to 'take a bit of beer and manure and rub it on the forehead.'

Arriving in tow upon the Ampney Crucis cricket field, the King of Spin had the appearance of 'Fantastic Mr Fox' in a slim fit sharp grey suit. His dyed groomed hair raised comment from a huge barrel of a man, aghast amongst the throng. 'Hell, he's gone as ginger as Ian Saxelby!'

A lady of a certain age nudged the barrel's elbow, 'I wouldn't have recognised him, you know. He looks nothing like he did on *X-Factor*.' I reflected on this - Shane Warne, Shane Ward, similar, similar. Lord, love us.

However, Shane's new look had indeed caused global mutters of cosmetic surgery. Poo-pooing the very idea, he claims he owes it all to 'new Estée Lauder moisturisers', a company Liz has a long-standing deal to endorse. On the down side, a monumental coughing spasm at the Rose Bowl a week earlier earned comment. News of the King's splutter in the *Guardian's* Nursery End column suggested he was as fond of 'the gaspers' as ever.

And there were soon hundreds of gaspers in front of the pavilion, and a half-dozen wearing green aprons and rubber gloves just inside the open doors. Shane, for whatever odd reason, had placed himself out of reach as Liz, with a beaming smile, stood at the top of the pavilion steps. She spoke nicely into a microphone before cutting the ceremonial ribbon and declaring the fête open.

Considerate folk with cameras clicked away from angles that managed to capture 'Dick Gearing' bit of the sign, but hide the offending double ells behind a veranda post. In cahoots with the *Mail,* the freelancer from *Barcroft Media* wasn't so inclined.

And maybe it was because Liz got distracted by the freelancer's lens that she came a gravitational cropper, stumbling skittle-skattle down the pavilion steps in her cork platform sandals, saving herself by last ditch grab at a handrail knob. Click-click-click-click-click went the camera before she had time to rearrange hair, poise and lemon curdled dress.

The *Mail* had its story, and it wasn't, as those in the pub had feared, about a spelling mistake.

Keeping his suit jacket as well as his shirt on, Shane got rid of possible frustration in failing to be a Sir Galahad by hurling wooden balls at a stacked plate shy. To the sound of smashing china he was heard to utter, 'that's a shame I need some plates at home'. This touched his Hurley girl. Best though, I thought, the great legend sticks to cricket balls, rather than wooden, or white tie and tiara ones.

Before finally taking their leave for the sanctuary of Liz's four hundred acres the couple had a dutiful bookstall rummage. Liz soon hobbled away with her man on one arm and crime writer Dick Francis' *Driving Force* tucked under her other.

Given the cricket loving stalwart of the community that Dick Gearing had once been, and the local hoo-hah about spell checks, the book title seemed somehow appropriate.

Pity though that the village's pot of Roman coins was now in Oxford's Ashmolean Museum. They must be worth a bob or two, and perfect for getting that memorial sign changed. I could only wish Ampney Crucis good luck with 'Gloucestershire Vibrant'.

TEN

Of Walls and Foundations

'You have not built a wall unless you have rounded a corner.'
Irish Proverb.

Chomping Double Gloucester on a Bath Oliver brought my anxiety back to the surface once more. I felt guilty. In cider dealing, I called it. The 1999 NatWest 'Cider Final' had tickled my sensibilities. My loyalties had become split. And I now feared a badgering in the Sett of Zum.

Overhead, above Taunton's County Ground, the late August sky was dark with thunderclouds. The Met Office talked about 'a percentage chance of precipitation', the sort of gobbledygook that would earn the weather service the Plain English Campaign's Golden Bull booby prize. In defence, a Met Office spokesman said: "Precipitation covers a wide range of stuff falling from the sky including rain, sleet, snow, hail, drizzle and even cats and dogs - but sums it up in just one word."

Fingers crossed, however, the start of the evening's T20 play between Zum and the Shire's Gladiators wouldn't get delayed. The truth be told, part of me hoped it would. There would be more sales potential. Three piles of my book about Zum cricket were stacked on the table in front of my nose. I sat poised, hopeful of signing a copy.

I didn't think the unassuming, bespectacled, grey bearded gentleman standing in his queue-of-one on the other side of the table knew who the hell I was. However, I knew by the Wyvern badge on his faded maroon sun hat that he was a home supporter, and probably had been one for many a forgettable season.

The sun hat helped himself to a book and starting leafing through it. He paused on a page and seemed to enjoy what he read. As his face creased into a smile I sensed an opening. He would do, I thought. I needed feedback on a delicate subject. 'I've just been asked to write a Gloucestershire book,' I said.

'Be slimmer than this one,' he quipped, abruptly putting the copy back down on top of the desk pile.

Gawd, I'd lost a sale. Well, in for penny in for a pound. 'What are *your* thoughts on Gloucestershire?'

'We should build a wall.' The sun hat obviously felt that he spoke for the whole of Zum.

I felt a bit edgy. 'Ah-ha. So, what if I actually *was* to write a book about Gloucestershire cricket?'

'You'd be put in the foundations.'

I never set out to cause upset. Yet, such a recent experience as this has shown me that when it comes to keypad tapping a book about West Country cricket one has to consider sensibilities, and tread ever so carefully, as if on eggshells. Important local rivalry requires it.

I reveal all this as almost fifteen years have now passed since I entered the grey stone world of Nevil Road through Grace' Gates to start filming 'Grace and Favour', the Shire's first venture into video merchandise. Uncle Tubby waggling his Brasher walking stick as a weapon of intimidation had persuaded me to broach the idea initially.

Now, as the sun hat turned his back on me a pop tune swirled irritatingly in the privacy of my head. *Handbags and Gladrags,* Mike d'Abo's catchy '60s song made contemporary by the Stereophonics, had morphed into 'kitbags and Gladirags'. It was common knowledge all was still not well in the Shire. Penury threatened.

With the club committee having heebie-jeebies over the budget, the start of 2011 season had seen comings and goings from the comfy armchairs in the players' dressing room. With Testing days behind him and taking his seat for T20s was a newly acquired Sri Lankan of high repute, the scary-eyed legend of the googly Muttiah Muralitharan.

Of the Irish, Will Porterfield had poddled off taking his bat to the Bears just as fiery barnet of Kevin O'Brien arrived. This aggressive right-handed middle to lower order basher comes from Ballsbridge in shadow of Lansdowne Road, a paddle sweep away from Dublin city centre. In early March he had achieved the world record for the fastest ever World Cup century. He had bludgeoned and wellied the exasperated English bowlers around Bengaluru's M. Chinnaswamy Stadium to reach his ton from a mere 50 deliveries, along the way hitting the longest six in the World Cup - the kind of player who likes to take the bull by the horns when he is in the mood.

The Shire's director of cricket, John Bracewell declared: "We are delighted to have signed Kevin to our squad with particular reference to his one-day skills. Given his heroics in the World Cup, the Gladiators have a genuine lion-slayer in their midst."

Kevin was probably licking his chops at the thought a summer ahead of marmal-izing English county attacks. Could he be anything other than nonplussed by the Jessop Tavern doom and gloom merchants? They were making pessimistic whis-perings about the Shire's unending descent into the black hole that is minor county cricket. As with their women counterparts languishing in Division 5 South and West, the Shire's chaps could soon be playing Buckinghamshire, Dorset and Wiltshire. And after that even Rutland might rear its head.

Indeed, to the consternation of the Jessop Tavern the fast bowling department had suffered a double whammy. Both Gemaal Hussain and the ginger-mopped, Steve Kirby with his tendency to get, according to Sky Sports Bumble aka David Lloyd, 'a little bit over-excited', had been lured from the cash-strapped Shire by nouveau riche Zum. Faith, therefore, had to be placed in a fingers-crossed relaunch of copper-bonce Mark 2 Ian Saxelby, grounded for the entire previous season with a dodgy shoulder.

What was needed was a leader with backbone.

Filling the role, and in need of a shave and a trim thirty-something Alex Gidman had, perhaps, taken inspiration from the stuff of, heroic historical fiction. 'Captain Giddo' had the appearance of a latter day Richard Sharpe. No one could accuse him of pusillanimity, even if the average bloke could spell the blooming word. Absolutely not.

In no way was Giddo a timid chap. Debuting for the county in 2002 and today more than 8,000 first-class runs to the good, he's one of the old guard and the cement of a team in transtion. Yet the woes of leadership were hanging heavy. Worse still, he had joined the walking wounded among his troops. There was need for a report, not of rifles in the Napoleonic sense, but something up to date about the efficacy of shot selections at Nevil Road and Cheltenham, and upon opposition pitches across fair England. And that included Taunton.

The augurs were not good.

Some Lines From History

'There've been some traumatic derbies between Gloucestershire and Somerset, in terms of once we had the ascendancy with Proctor and Zaheer and then it was grabbed away from us in the era of Botham, Richards and Garner. We've played a lot of games where the opposition on one side or the other had one comfortably. And there have been very few really close fixtures.'

David Graveney, Gloucestershire, Somerset and Durham.

Now TV cameras catch 'every blink' of a Test Match; umpires with light meters; cricketers hung around with jewellery, embracing the fall of a wicket and engaging in other preposterous histrionics; batsmen and fielders in helmets, padded in every part of the anatomy, bowlers in bandeaux; all against a background of moronic chanting and rattling beer cans. Yesterday has gone.'

Grahame Parker, *Gloucestershire Road* (1983).

ELEVEN

For The Love Of Apples

'There! You see? It's always like that with these West Countrymen;
they bowl superbly for an hour or so, and then they begin to think about apples.'
C.B. Fry (Cricketer, diplomat and writer, 1872-1956).

It was going to be packed. 7000 bums on seats were estimated. I took out my biro and scrumpled Moleskine notebook and wandered amongst the fast growing Taunton crowd to gather jottings and pearls of wisdom. Somewhere amongst the throng were Goose and Mona. Both wore rain jackets hiding polo shirts bearing the Shire badge.

Mona had a habit of speaking her mind a little too loudly. Her 'O'Brien's going to moider these buggers,' caused a scowl or two in the jostle; and 'Murali's going to befuddle their wee fundaments,' earned quizzical stares.

Maybe, such latter glances arose out of the confusion as to which 'Murali' Mona actually meant. Both sides had one. Obviously, she had in her mind Muralitharan of the Shire, the non-drinker who confessed to know little about cider other that it 'encouraged noise', and was 'good for a game of twenty/twenty'.

Zum on the other hand had Murali Kartik. And he was a very different twirlyman character.

'Hey love, save confusion, better you call ours 'Muttiah',' urged Goose.

I had to agree. This, I supposed, was just the set of circumstance the Sri Lankan might have preferred this alternative. Although Muttiah might sooner have had Kartik's generous contract. So keen had Zum been to sign the former Indian Test star that his contract basically said he could get anything he asked for, including a bicycle for his wife. Such enforceable niceties would never do for the impecunious Shire.

Of course, Goose and Mona were rooting for the visitors to do the double - a tad of solace in a meagre 2011 campaign that had prompted Captain Giddo to say: 'Although we want to win every game, there is a large element of development in what we are doing this season. Whatever the outcome it will be more great experience for our young players.'

A week earlier Goose and Mona had danced a polka. I cast my mind back to the moment.

On the first evening of July Nevil Road's version of India's great dragonfly migration had seen furry-bodied moths with the appearance of winged hobbit goats fluttering pitch side. They fled an immense smoke pall emanating from the popular burger stall that sat close to the boundary edge of the county circuit's second largest playing area. Minding my health I crunched on a supermarket pippin before coughing pith.

Perhaps, to the uninitiated, apples are apples. But it's all about where they originate. When it comes to red or white ball battles between the cider counties of the Shire and Zum differences have long been divisive. Not that there were any red ball tussles these days. The Shire floundered in Division Two of the County Championship. Zum were the hoi polloi thoroughbreds of Division One.

Today, only in the white ball game of T20 or CB 40 one-dayers do the two teams encounter one another for bragging rights, the Shire considered underdogs by cricket's media.

Contrary to Cotswold opinion the cliché 'to the slaughter' didn't mean visiting the 'Thankful Village'. For if one believes the translations of academia, Upper Slaughter translates as 'muddy place', derived from the Saxon word *Slohtre*, where, 'keeping your Eye in' was not about net practice, but rather the need for monitoring the level of the local river. To be on the safe side, one might reach for sandbags filled with the spoils of the Nevil Road square. The pitches created upon it were, in the words of ex-players, 'sand pits'.

Fitting then, that Gladiators should bless them.

However, the new era that first cloaked the Shire in 2002 has, so far, not proved very auspicious. Obviously, budget restrictions are taken into account as supporters gird their loins and continue to do their bit.

Take, for example, the gladiatorial helmet. Showing talents worthy of *Blue Peter*, the less seriously minded brethren, like Goose and Mona, took to wear a floppy sun hat with two shoelaces attached to the brim. With the brim pulled down over the ears the shoelace ends were knotted together under the chin. And, mimicking an heroic plume, a paintbrush, its bristles stiff with dried blue paint, was shoved by its handle into the sun hat's hatband.

If this wasn't enough, and as if taking a leaf out of my Uncle Tubby's book, less innovative fans had taken to wearing one-dimensional Roman helmet masks made of cardboard.

Collectively, the intent was there to help rouse the spirits of a team of wee willy winkies wearing blue pyjamas under the high wattage lights of the Bristolian night.

The knowing Goose commented that wicket-to-wicket the batting strip was 'more of a bumpy, not to say, dusty road than usual'. Umpires Peter Willey and Neil Mallender both raised eyebrows. This was not the sort of surface for fluid stroke play that pampered Zum were used to on their home turf.

Winning the toss and batting first, the visitors' innings became a low scoring shambles due in no small part to the off-spin of the diminutive debutant, Banbury-born teenager Jack Taylor. Jack the lad twiddled out Zum's middle order taking 4 for16, including bowling the hard-hitting West Indian journey-man-cum-cricket mercenary Kieron Pollard before he chanced to cause any mayhem.

The Shire's response was 'watchful' in the early overs. Too much so. Several Shire wickets tumbled in a cluster. The Shire were suddenly 18 for 3, all the wickets to pacey Zum whippersnapper Lewis Gregory.

'Here we go again,' came the groans. Such pessimism, Mounting scoreboard pressure led to ongoing jitters until the match turned on a risky run born of desperation. Do-or-die Jack had not only bowled as if he had benefitted from a Murilitheran blood infusion, he had also the top scored in the Shire's innings. His was a let the Devil take hindmost attitude that required many a scamper and a trust in Lady Luck.

Having edged-cum-trickled a Pollard medium-fast pacer back in the direction it had come the optimistic youth was only halfway down the pitch pelting to the danger end, bat outstretched, by the time Pollard had the ball in hand, the stumps almost within his touching distance. With seemingly enough time to read a novella, 'Polly' took careful aim and released the ball underarm with muscle. The majority of the crowd gave a groan of resignation. Zum supporters held their breath. Followed a nanosecond later by an incredulous exhalation.

Pollard made an absolute horlicks of it.

Overthrows! Perhaps he was put off by one of the winged goats.

'Oh, you gurt numpty!' yelled a maginalised mingler.

'GLAWSTER!' bellowed most of the host.

An under-armed 'exocet' may have stiffed a mutt at Lord's once, but no pooch expired from Pollard's throw. Instead, the dog had its day. The Shire won with three balls to spare. The Shire faithful joined Jack Taylor in dreamland. A broadsheet next day summarized the match with a one liner: 'Gloucestershire 124-8 (19.3 overs) beat Somerset 121-9 (20 overs) by two wickets'. The sports editor possibly thought there was no need for greater detail, or to debate whether the South Group's second-from-bottom side turning over second-from top was a shock.

The Shire had bucked the trend, and defied the pre-match doom merchant fore-casts of Giddo's saplings being 'Pollarded'. As it turned out victory over Marcus Trescothick's Zum was 'Taylored' to perfection, and to a man the Gladiators were given the thumbs up. And Goose and Mona danced their polka.

And so here I was in Taunton. The teams were to do battle again. The weight of expectation would have to contend with feared weight of water. Local advice was to let players run about on the pitch to let off as much steam as possible. It was for the best, it was said. There were still sniggers emanating from the Zum dress-ing room about the recent visit of Dominic Cork's Hampshire. That particular load of hogs had earned reputation of being a pretty wild bunch. And too much wet stuff on that day was the precursor to embarrassment.

With mallards swimming in the outfield, and a report of fishing cormorant, play was called off without a ball being bowled. Liberated hogs sallied forth for a night on the Taunton tiles. Not finding much in the way of entertainment that damp mid week they decided to create their own by using the 'resources' available to them.

Their anonymous ringleader had the jolly wheeze that they should all try to 'get off 'with, and I hesitate to say this, ladies of more mature years. The rules were simple. The chap taken home by the oldest woman, and able to have his way with her, won. Simple. Most of the Hants lads were up for the challenge.

However, in a rumour that spread like wildfire, the jape backfired on one of their number. An upper order batsman, unwittingly described by Shaun Udal on Sky Sports as 'the finished article, polished in everything he does,' and 'class person-ified,' yet who shall remain nameless, found himself locked inside the house of a desperate housewife.

The unfortunate cricketer only managed to escape lascivious clutches by squirming through the bathroom window. At two o'clock in the early hours he wandered Taunton's quiet puddled streets dressed only in a towel, and completely lost. One could wonder if his red face came from a winner's glow of pride.

The Shire's young impressionables on the other hand were kept on the straight and narrow, closely monitored by their Kiwi coach John Bracewell. His was a proud surname in New Zealand sport and eyes were already focusing on the latest addition - the swing bowling qualities of John's nephew, Doug.

John 's bold outlook and uncompromising approach opened players' eyes and helped the team take its game forward. The players responded to him and deserved credit for wanting to change. His main demand is each player be 'in the zone', but has admitted that 'it's difficult to get all eleven players in the zone at one time'. Two or three would be a start, was the current opinion of Jessop Taverners.

Well, at least John had got eleven to Taunton's damp but drying sward. And he could dangle a carrot - bragging rights. Back-to-back T20 wins over Zum were a modern rarity.

The Taunton after-workers began drifting in with the mizzle. The throng was joined by a smattering of more folk from up the M5 arriving incognito through Somerset County Ground's high, wide gates dedicated to legends 'Farmer' White and Sir Vivian Richards, and the ironic Joel Garner short, narrow gate.

The locals looked apprehensively skywards and muttered about a badly draining outfield. The majority of Shire supporters wore furrows on their brows for different reasons. Lean angst ridden times also meant cash flow was a greater problem than run trickle. There was no reason, however, not to make a beeline for the bar, adding to the urban myth that Twenty20 attracted football-like crowds whose intention it was to guddle as much as humanely possible within two hours.

Towards the tail of the queue came the evening's first chunterings of calamity. Still with almost half an hour until the first was to be bowled in anger an administrative error or tragic oversight led me jotting a note into my black Moleskine notebook: '5.05. Cider's run out. Should have ordered double.'

At the shorter queue for scorecards Goose dug deep into his pockets for the change only to discover a second calamity, although one not so unexpected as cider famine. Still, his furrowed brow seemed to suffer a heavier plough, or even a shell blast of Waterloo. Scanning the batting order Goose's worst fears were confirmed. There was no Captain Giddo.

He was still crocked so John Bracewell had 'elevated' his fellow countryman Kane Williamson to be captain for the day. Although, to be fair, 'elevated' was the wrong word. Especially true given the estimate of Kane's height so earnestly provided by his international teammate Jacob Oram. Jacob felt the need to explain during a post-match dissection how his spectacular catch of South Africa's Jacques Kallis at deep midwicket had come about. 'Thankfully,' he said 'I'm six foot six, and I replaced Kane Williamson who, I think, is four foot six.' With Kane now the size of a hobbit the Shire could begin to be confused with Tolkein's Middle Earth.

If this all wasn't enough, to prevail against Zum the Shire would have to adapt to a Taunton playing surface that was the inverse of Bristol's. Yes, the wicket was great. Shame about the previous winter's newly laid outfield. As surfaces go it resembled a brand of expensively furrowed potato crisps. Throughout the season so far many a fielder had been in dismay, and derided of his teammates, as the ball bobbled through his legs after hitting the wrong end of a rut.

There was little of cheer. Not even fancy dress. I put it down to the Taunton crowd rushing straight from work. No time to become auk or elf, fluffy fresian cow or designer-stubbled nun. The proud owners of cardboard gladiatorial helmets wisely left them back up the M5 for fear of them getting soggy. There were, however, the Zum abundance of flimsy yellow plastic hard hats upon the heads of young and old - a marketing gimmick highlighting the destructive potential of captain Marcus Trescothick's merry band of tonkers.

Indeed, by swinging those blunt weapons of destruction so ably 'Somerset Tonkers' had a certain ring about it. Better this, perhaps, than the 'Sabres' tag that had gone, leaving just plain 'Somerset'. Goose and Mona agreed this was down to Zum having lost their cutting edge in pressure situations. But there were also whispers that dropping the name was a knee-jerk reaction to a quip from Shire skipper Mark Alleyne during the floodlight pre-match banter in the corresponding fixture back in 2004. In the glare of Sky TV cameras and asked about Zum's chances, Mark had scoffed 'They're only the Scabbers.' Mostly aptly had Mark earned his nickname 'Boo Boo'.

His quip relayed live to the crowd via Zum's loudspeaker system roused many a boo and grumble of local self-righteous indignation, although by the game's end Mark's cheeky confidence had found basis. Neil Burns' failing Zum outfit got bludgeoned, the Shire winning by whopping margin of 8 wickets.

Oh, but how times had changed in a few short years. The boot, fully repaired had been laced, tied and was firmly on the other foot. Today, the Gladiators had become the underdogs. One could almost hear Laurie Lee playing his violin upon the oppressive dark clouds overhead. And who could blame him. His had been the world of the interwar years. Those when the homegrown son of Apperley, Alfred Dipper, Caterham's Bev Lyon, and, of course, that Kentish lad of Buckland, Wally Hammond, entertained.

Out on the field it was time for the players to maybe begin their warm-up on the announcement that Kane Williamson had won the toss and would 'have a bowl'. The only sensible decision given the aforementioned clouds

At the far side of the ground from where Goose, Mona and I stood Zum took the field not with practice bats but with a football, and began to show off their skills to spectators filling the Marcus Trescothick and Sir Ian Botham stands. Wearing a yellow bib, Peter Trego began to dribble.

Gazing out across the field, some cautionary words of former India captain and Zum opener Sunil Gavaskar came to back me: 'Somebody should tell them nobody from Manchester United, Arsenal and Liverpool has come to scout talent here.' One of Sunny's top gripes was cricketers injuring themselves playing other sports during practice.

No such danger from the Shire boys. They were mostly huddled in the dug out, with the odd exceptions. Muttiah was nowhere to be seen. And in the nets in front of the old pavilion, and with what the untutored eye might take to be a pet dog's flexible plastic ball launcher, John Bracewell hooned white leather at the angelic looking newly wed, Hamish Marshall. His Shire cap perched on a head of Medici curls, Hamish, perhaps, offered a Renaissance of hope - until Bracewell gave him one around the lughole to keep him honest. However, by showing the full face of his favourite Boom Boom bat, Hamish seemed intent in perfecting the Brigadier block, and being a resistance fighter.

Goose gave me a nudge and nodded towards the activity. 'That's a Sidearm – the pro version.'

'You what?'

'The cricket ball thrower. It's the latest thing. You can easily whang the ball up to 90 miles an hour. Pretty rapid.'

Hamish proceeded to edge two in a row. 'They should start calling him 'Nickoff,' I chirped.

'Maybe. Mona's begun calling him "Doodah". Haven't you love?' Goose turned to grin at his partner.

'Are two quick wickets known as a Twix?' said Mona, innocently in the sweetest Irish accent.

'Why Doodah?' I asked.

Goose wasn't short in coming forward. 'Some bright spark's bin pratting about on

Wikipedia.'

'Oh, do tell,' I said.

Goose snorted. 'Probably inspired by Hamish letting on that his funniest moment in cricket was brushing his hair into an afro during a 20 over bash. He's been renamed "Hashim Doodah de Davide".'

'Really? Dangerous, dangerous. Wait till someone taps in 'Hashish'. That'll get the rumour mill rumbling good and proper. Anyway, aren't things weird enough as they are, given his passport. He's already under the spell of the leprechauns.'

It certainly seemed as if Hamish was. After his late call-up for the 2007 Cricket World Cup, and scoring one tournament half-century, he chose to reject a contract with New Zealand in order to play for the Shire. Due to holding an Irish passport Hamish didn't count as an overseas player, just so long as he doesn't play for New Zealand. But still the history books will always say he and his twin brother James were the first identical pair to play Test cricket.

For the obvious reason Hamish was easy to identify, not so with the rest of the team. Yes, names and numbers where on back of shirts but not on the back of their sweaters. Nominated by Hamish as the worst dressed bloke of Shire, lanky quickie David Payne did stand out above the rest. With him, perhaps more than Muttiah, rested the chalice of hope. The previous year, his 7 for 29 against Essex at Chelmsford were pretty damned decent. Just as Zum put their football away he began to practice turning his left-arm over. Mona was quick to notice. 'The Payne o'Poole will surly cause them the flibberty jibbits,' she said.

He did. Trescothick out, off stump uprooted second ball for a duck. Cue a pregnant pause of deathly silence, loudly broken by Goose. 'Ha ha ha!'

This was unfortunate. Mona gave Goose an almighty shove. "Gawd's sake, wind yer neck in!' But she was too late. Needled into cussedness, Zum dug deep to preserve their vaulted reputation. By the interval between innings they had set a challenging total of 170.

In reply Marshall and O'Brien gave the Shire's chase a rollicking start by giving it some humpty.

'Bonecrusher' Kirby got the run around, and it wasn't graceful. Arms pumping, body straining, he chased leather, busting a gut until he was puce in the face. Whenever he managed to haul up the ball Goose and Mona, with the full force their lungs, shouted 'GLAWSTERRRRRR!'

The glares Kirby sent their way were received with good humour and with relish.

'You wouldn't think Kirbs' such a pussy cat off the field,' chuckled Goose.

I had to smile, too, remembering Sky pundit Mark Butcher's remark: 'On the pitch Kirby goes a bit mad.' That was an understatement, but he's one of those players who's like gold dust. Giving up a benefit to go and play for Zum, and never likely to get a full England cap, he gave his new club a hundred per cent. And why change a habit? He'd done exactly the same for the Shire, Old Bristolians, and Yorkshire before that.

Slowly Goose and Mona spirits began to ebb. The Zum bowlers chipped away, catches were held, and the run rate choked. In the battle of the Muralies, Kartik, bicycle or no bicycle, won the day. For the Shire there was no double. Goose and Mona danced no polka. The Shire Gloucestershire had slipped to a 15-run defeat.

John Bracewell was far from despondent. 'A few little things settled the match in Somerset's favour,' he remarked. 'But for 90 per cent of the game we played very well.

'We had to bowl with a wet ball, which probably meant our spinners were less effective than they might have been. But we also have to give Somerset credit because they bowled and fielded well at key stages of the match.

'Overall I think the future of West country cricket looked bright.'

Well said, sir, I thought. JB's last point was the important one to know.

A few days later, shortly after I had learned Jack Taylor had oddly nominated Marcus Trecothick as his dream captain, De Doodah Davide reverted back to 'Hamish John Hamilton' Marshall on Wikipedia. The status quo had returned on some counts.

'Cricket to me is summer and summer is cricket. The crack of the bat against the ball amid the buzzing and humming of summer sounds is to still to me a note of pure joy.'

Lucy Baldwin, 1st issue of *Women's Cricket*, 1930.

TWELVE

Of Jam and Roses

'A rose is a rose is a rose.'

Proverb.

I had set off early up the M5, so hopefully giving myself plenty of time to see Kent roll over and have their tummy tickled. Unfortunately I didn't seem to be going anywhere. The culprit, a C-reg Ford Fiesta Finesse rust bucket, smoked rubber-neck entertainment.

The tedium of being stuck behind a caravan in a traffic jam of inestimable length allows the mind to wander. Mine began with a calculation. C-reg ... that's um, 19.... 88. No, no, no ... 86. 1986! The year of Roddy's happiest cricketing moment.

I'd met him whilst recording documentary 'vox pops'. But when the Hell was that? Certainly, it was Cheltenham on a Sunday. The umpires wore smart light blue blazers. And just so folk knew which team was which, 'Gloucestershire' or 'Lancashire' was emblazoned across the middle of multi coloured shirts. Woodland green, white and red, played navy blue, white and red.

Without having reached double figures, Michael Atherton at the top of the red rose order had a nibble outside the off stump. Quick as a flash Jack Russell dived low to his left before popping to his feet, ball in glove, to enjoy the departure. Mike Smith, claimed to be the foremost exponent of swing bowling in county cricket in the 90s, had got another scalp, and, quite possibly, owed Jack more teabags.

And so departed 'Athers', Jack's former England captain. Later, in his retirement Athers commented that one of the things he failed to miss was 'that dirty, smelly, grubby, patched-up, stitched-up, upside-down-flowerpot-of-a-thing that perched atop Jack's straggly hair throughout his career'. That particular object of attire caused Athers more grief as England skipper than any Brian Lara hundred or Shane Warne hat-trick.

An extract of Athers diary covering England's 1998 tour of the West Indies appeared in the *Telegraph*:

> Atherton: *'Jack, will you wear an England cap?'*
> Russell: *'No.'*
> Atherton: *'Is there any way we can find a compromise solution?'*
> Russell: *'No.'*
> Stewart: *'Well, if Jack's going to wear his hat, I'm going to wear my white, not blue, helmet.'*
> Hussain: *'If the Gaffer's going to wear his white helmet I'd like to wear my favourite baseball cap to field in.'*

A happy compromise was reached in the end. Jack stitched the England logo on to his beloved hat.

And, amongst the throngs of Gloucestershire supporters at Cheltenham I remembered other microcosms of detail. A young boy and girl messed around, absorbed in a game of tennis ball cricket in between the main chapel door and massed bloom of white roses in their beds. There were also prams, an absurd timeworn brimless straw hat, and glasses of white wine being sun-warmed on summer brown grass.

I wracked my brain before visualising Roddy in a hurry to catch what was left of the afternoon's play. He was a kind faced, balding, chubby, thirty-something, blinking behind gold-rimmed sunglasses, his white shirt's top button unfastened, and work tie at half-mast. And, he was perspiring.

My having blocked his way to the bar, Roddy had looked at me pleadingly. But he remained courteous as I quizzed him about his take on the whole Cheltenham Festival experience.

He sighed, gave a longing gaze towards the beer tent, and then gave his full attention to my camera's red recording light. 'Cheltenham's number one for me, the best of the cricket festivals.' he managed to enthuse. 'The cricket's wonderful, there's a sociable holiday feel.' He gave another glance towards the bar, and then one out to the middle where Shire opener Tony Wright was batting in the competent manner that would earn him the most one-day centuries by any Englishman for the county.

Roddy began to fidget. Smiling reassurance, I asked him for his greatest Cheltenham memory.

His reply was immediate. '86, we beat Hampshire. Their team was crammed with household names - Gordon Greenidge, Paul Terry, Robin Smith, Malcolm Marshall. Wow. They only needed about 110 to win. Courtney and Syd bowled them out for less than 100, and we went 50 points clear at the top of the Championship in the last week of July.'

Paul Terry was German, born in Osnabrück, I recollected as a police car pelted along the hard shoulder. Nil desperandum. The driver in the static estate car beside me began thumping his steering wheel with clenched fists. Those on the back seat I assumed to be his three kids weren't singing *'the wheels on the bus'* any more as his 'wife' reached to close the electric windows. I tried hard to not to show any amusement. The best way was to distract myself.

David Lawrence, the great 'Syd', I reflected. His Caribbean parents really did produce one big hulk of a trooper, and a Gloucester boy to boot. With arms and legs always skittle-skattle as he hurtled towards the bowling crease, Syd was capable of bowling both with extreme pace and with extreme inaccuracy, often simultaneously.

But sometimes he got speed and direction right, and never more so than on a glorious evening at the Wagon Works in 1985 when, on a good track, he and Courtney ripped Yorkshire apart for 83. His boyhood friends were there and they enveloped him as he left the field, a champion from their own streets. Soon the whole of England had wanted to adopt him.

Then in February 1992, when he was 28, Syd was carried screaming in agony from the pitch during England's third Test against New Zealand. His left kneecap had split in two as his 17-stone frame brought his front foot thudding into the Wellington turf. The noise of the injury reached as far as the boundary; spectators said the sound was 'like a pistol shot'.

Having once wanted to be a boxer Syd was a fighter and 13 months of hard slog, self-doubt and pain followed as he battled to recover his fitness. By March 1993, his benefit year, he hoped to begin the new season with Gloucestershire.

Then cruel fate struck. Syd was doing some simple exercises, when fractured his kneecap again, though not quite as severely. His choice was blatant: give up - or fight back. Syd being Syd he chose the latter. And at beginning of August '93, 3,000 people held their breath at Cheltenham College as a David Lawrence XI took on the Rest of the World. Syd set off to cover the 25 yards to the crease, clearly favouring his left leg. At delivery, he brought his front foot up high, then down. The ball strayed down the leg side and went for a single, but no one, least of all Syd seemed to mind. He continued his follow-through for a further 10 yards then turned round with a smile. And 3,000 breathed again.

An over or two later and he was producing some cheeky bouncers. Sadly the comeback was brief. No Shire cricketer tried harder. And in that second inning against Hampshire, Syd took four wickets to Courtney's six.

Roddy had been wistful when he said: 'I really, really thought that day that we'd won the County Championship. My ambition is to see us win it, just once in my lifetime. I'd die a happy man if that were to happen.'

Click. Wright was bowled by Watkinson. Enter Monty Lynch to join Aussie Andrew Symonds. Roddy had made his excuses.

Oh, but what year was it? Courtney was definitely still around, regretfully not so much Syd.

Then, I recalled Peter West, relaxed in an open necked shirt and green pullover, sat on a comfy floral pattern sofa, an array of Toby jugs regimented along his lounge mantelpiece behind him. Our conversation had got onto the subject of the Cheltenham pitch.

'No one could blame Gloucestershire for it,' Peter had said, 'but those twenty-two yards seemed to have a little bit more grass on. The purpose was purely to suit Courtenay, etcetera.'

Anyway, this, it turned out, hadn't been the traditional way of things.

Peter began making slow bowling actions while twiddling his fingers.
'Interesting thing about Cheltenham, when I was young, was Charlie Parker's slow left arm, and Tom Goddard off-spinner. In those days the Cheltenham pitch, naturally, wasn't made too green. It was made to take a bit of spin. And they both did pretty well on it.'

Peter had chuckled, almost to himself.

'I didn't see Charlie, but all Gloucestershire knew that he was the greatest slow left-armer in England. A radical rather than a socialist, Charlie was one of David Foot's "Cricket's Unholy Trinity". If memory serves me right, the other two were Jack MacBryan and Cecil Parkin.'

Charlie had a crusty exterior but a kind heart. His 3,278 first-class wickets where deserving of more than his one Test cap. But he could be an awkward character, and rub his social superiors up the wrong way, which, as a labourer's son from Prestbury, meant just about everyone.

One day in the lift at Bristol's Grand Hotel, he grabbed Plum Warner, the chairman of selectors, by the coat lapels and told him in no uncertain terms what he thought of him.

His did, however, keep the best of himself for the pitch. In 1930, he bowled the Shire to a famous tie with the Australians. He dismissed Bradman in both innings. The Shire's skipper Bev Lyon is quoted a saying. 'Any captain can win or lose a game against the Australians, but there are bloody few who can tie one.' For his part, the Don never played at Bristol again. On such days, Robertson-Glasgow reckoned, Charlie could make any opponent 'look like a child batting with a pencil'.

Peter West moved his own thoughts on. 'I saw Tom Goddard, with his enormous hands, at the end of his career. Believe it or not, he started as a fast bowler. Dennis Compton used to give him fearful stick with the sweep shot that drove him into distraction. My God, he was still a good bowler, though.'

But hey, I thought, Mike Smith was a good bowler, too. And, like Charlie Parker, enough of one to play a single Test for England. Mike got his cap at Headingley in 1997 against Australia. Surely this qualified him as being, in Peter's words, 'etcetera'. So anyway, that meant I'd met Roddy in 1995, which would put him in his 50s, now. Blimey, how time flies.

Good Heavens, I realised the caravan in front of me was speeding away.

GLOUCESTERSHIRE v HAMPSHIRE

Britannic Assurance County Championship 1986
Venue: College Ground, Cheltenham 2nd, 4th, 5th August 1986 (3-day match)
Toss: Hampshire won the toss and decided to field
Umpires: AA Jones, R Palmer

Gloucestershire first innings

PW Romaines	c Parks	b Tremlett	10
KP Tomlins	c CL Smith	b Tremlett	10
CWJ Athey	lbw	b Tremlett	42
P Bainbridge	c Greenidge	b Connor	22
AW Stovold	c Parks	b Connor	17
KM Curran	c RA Smith	b Marshall	25
JW Lloyds	c CL Smith	b Marshall	35
+RC Russell	c Parks	b James	16
*DA Graveney	not out		7
CA Walsh	lbw	b Marshall	0
DV Lawrence	c Parks	b James	0

Extras (2 b, 6 lb, 7 nb, 2 w)   17
Total (all out, 63.4 overs)   201

Fall of wickets:
1-19, 2-26, 3-87, 4-109, 5-132, 6-151, 7-184, 8-197, 9-200, 10-201 (63.4 ov)

Hampshire bowling	Overs	Mdns	Runs	Wkts
Marshall	19	4	42	3
Connor	20	4	63	2
Tremlett	15	2	55	3
James	9.4	3	33	2

Hampshire first innings

CG Greenidge	lbw	b Lawrence	38
VP Terry	c Bainbridge	b Walsh	0
TC Middleton	c Russell	b Walsh	27
CL Smith	not out		72
RA Smith	c Lloyds	b Walsh	25
+RJ Parks	c Lawrence	b Walsh	0
*MCJ Nicholas	c Curran	b Walsh	25
KD James	run out		1
MD Marshall	c Walsh	b Lawrence	3
TM Tremlett	c Athey	b Bainbridge	52
CA Connor	c Russell	b Walsh	0
Extras	(8 b, 9 lb, 10 nb)		27
Total	(all out, 94 overs)		270

Fall of wickets:
1-1, 2-71, 3-75, 4-124, 5-124, 6-134, 7-148, 8-157, 9-269, 10-270 (94 ov)

Gloucestershire bowling	Overs	Mdns	Runs	Wkts
Walsh	33	12	90	6
Lawrence	29	7	92	2
Bainbridge	20	3	42	1
Graveney	10	5	18	0
Lloyds	2	0	11	0

Gloucestershire second innings

PW Romaines	c Middleton	b Marshall	0
KP Tomlins		b James	30
CWJ Athey	c Parks	b Connor	36
P Bainbridge	c RA Smith	b Marshall	21
AW Stovold	lbw	b James	48
KM Curran	c RA Smith	b James	14
JW Lloyds		b James	0
+RC Russell	c Terry	b James	9
*DA Graveney	not out		2

CA Walsh	b Marshall		3
DV Lawrence	b Marshall		0
Extras (1 b, 18 lb, 2 nb)			21
Total (all out, 65 overs)			184

Fall of wickets:
1-0, 2-55, 3-96, 4-102, 5-147, 6-148, 7-178, 8-179, 9-184, 10-184 (65 ov)

Hampshire bowling	Overs	Mdns	Runs	Wkts
Marshall	22	6	44	4
Connor	12	0	44	1
Tremlett	15	4	43	0
James	16	4	34	5

Hampshire second innings

CG Greenidge	c Athey	b Lawrence	26
VP Terry		b Walsh	13
TC Middleton	c Athey	b Lawrence	1
RA Smith		b Walsh	23
*MCJ Nicholas	c Romaines	b Walsh	7
KD James	c Graveney	b Walsh	6
MD Marshall	c Athey	b Walsh	5
TM Tremlett	c Russell	b Lawrence	3
+RJ Parks	c Curran	b Lawrence	4
CL Smith	c Curran	b Walsh	5
CA Connor	not out		0
Extras (5 nb)			5
Total (all out, 32.5 overs)			98

Fall of wickets:
1-39, 2-39, 3-63, 4-69, 5-74, 6-83, 7-88, 8-92, 9-97, 10-98 (32.5 ov)

Gloucestershire bowling	Overs	Mdns	Runs	Wkts
Walsh	16.5	5	34	6
Lawrence	16	2	64	4

Gloucestershire won by 17 runs.

THIRTEEN

Graffiti and Oddball Palette

'I continue to get further away from the usual painter's
tools such as easel, palette, brushes, etcetera, I prefer sticks.'
Jackson Pollock (Painter, 1912-1956).

The scenery had been magnificent. The rocky slopes, decorated by purple-blossomed Judas trees and carpets of wild flowers, grazed by goats, and hovered over by golden eagles, were the stuff of artistic inspiration. Edward Lear, of nonsense rhyme fame, once set up his easel in this spot as he painted and portrayed the island of Corfu in watercolour. Here, in the ruined and all but deserted mountain village of Ano Perithia, the schoolhouse walls were scrawled with graffiti. 'The Czech Republic' and 'Hanna, Köln' vied with 'Bev n Dave'.

Carefully opening four bottles of lively homemade ginger beer, the dogged owner of a small precipice teetering bar butted in on the cricket chitchat between my wife and I and our friends Gareth and Chris. 'In Corfu everyone knows cricket. It's been there since 1824,' he informed us.

After a pause the thin resident tomcat scritched behind an ear then plaintively miaowed news that we chose to ignore.

It was old hat on learning Greece, granted Affiliate Membership of the ICC in 1995, is using cricket to promote harmony. And down in Corfu Town traffic growls by the graffiti art daubed on a high roadside wall where Banksy, son of Bristol, has added a contribution. His figure in a bandana throwing flowers carries the message: 'Our goals are our dreams'. A motto, I'd thought, suitable for adoption by Gloucestershire was also fitting for the Greeks.

There were ambitions of qualifying for the cricket World Cup 2040 with a team comprising mainly of Corfiots. Step up the future players of Gymnastikos CC, Feax CC, and Kerkyra CC. To help hone Hellenic skills, the Greek national side had recently played the MCC in a Twenty20 clash, and primary school kids now played Kwik Cricket on the site of Nero's Mint.

Now, my wife and I, too, were in Corfu Town having asked Gareth and Chris to show us the English cricket pitch. The location of the historical legacy was intriguing - a lime tree shaded clover covered space between the statue of Lawrence Durrell, lauded in his lifetime as the world's greatest authority on sex, and tall Venetian houses, in faded Twenty20 colours, lean as wicket widths, though perhaps slightly jaded by long years of civilized amateur enjoyment.

In what, to Gareth, seems like an age ago since buying a few *stremata* totalling about an acre of Corfu and a terrace view of Albania, he'd done the sensible thing in learning a smattering of the lingo. However, he readily admitted to not showing the slightest inkling toward groundsmanship. Hidden in the garden grass a small sign pegged beneath a olive tree read: 'I fought the lawn and the lawn won'. Indeed, it would surprise me if he'd given his bushy grey beard much of a trim since his island arrival, either. As a result his wiry frame topped by a smart Panama hat appeared a tad top heavy.

His diminutive partner Chris, her face a smile of freckles, expressed in her broad West Country burr that Greek was Greek and, as a language, best left well alone. And, despite her having driven 'Doris', a double-decker bus, around Bristol for many years, she lacked the confidence to drive of the battered and electrically eccentric family Skoda. So she'd delegated the responsibility to Gareth.

What the couple had in common was to regularly check the cricket scores via the Internet. Yet, even here they deferred to be different. Naturally, with Gareth being a Welshman, he clicked in on Glamorgan, whereas Chris did similar for the Shire.

And bearing in mind Hellenic harmony, Gareth had just about stopped gloating over *that* Gladiators defeat, arguably their heaviest suffered since T20 was first introduced. Glamorgan Dragons had romped to victory with six overs to spare to complete a humiliating 10-wicket annihilation. A day Ian Harvey, it's said, forlornly cuddled his fluffy Sky Sports microphone as if it were a comfort toy.

'No cricket here, today,' I said matter-of-factly, watching another English legacy, a brass band, struggle to unload a tuba from a bus crammed with instruments before laying the gurt object down gently on the outfield.

'Do you know, without his blooming beard I used to think Gareth reminded me of Jack Russell,' laughed Chris.

'Really? Even with Gareth's dapper titfer?' I responded, before going on to cause a slight misunderstanding that wasn't quite my fault.

Gareth thought I'd said, 'Of course Jack's really arsy'. I meant, the eccentric talent from Stroud was christened 'R. C.' which translates as Robert Charles. I didn't interrupt as Chris sorted the matter out.

Yet, when it came to making comparisons, one has to admit that Gareth was known locally as man of brush and paint. Unlike Edward Lear, Gareth had brushes of the larger variety, and are ones he uses to daub a painter and decorator's emulsion. So, which of whom Jack Russell, 23-years a Gloucestershire cricketer, would have identified wasn't really open to debate.

Jack, 5ft 8in and 9st 8lb with his boots on, had always struck me as an easily recognizable character, and I defer to the description given by Ian Henderson of the *Telegraph* who wrote in 1999: 'In his floppy hat and dark glasses, Russell resembles nothing so much as a Flowerpot Man who has walked on to the set of Easy Rider.' But, of course, that was when he was doing his stuff behind the stumps.

On the occasions I happened to meet up with him he always appeared incognito.

At the Grace Centenary Dinner, Jack in black bowtie and tuxedo, looked as out of place as a penguin on the moon. I mentioned this as I shook his flipper.

A week or so later I was in an Art Gallery along Chipping Sodbury High Street. Without a flowerpot to hand, or indeed any of the customary clobber of his summer trade, the well-groomed and moustached artist in the British Lions rugby shirt gestured toward a watercolour of dawn rising over misty Gloucestershire meadows. 'I painted this in … 1994,' he said.

The painting, soothing on the eye, hung beside others of similar ilk depicting a pastoral Cotswolds, like the one of stonewalling along a winding lane, or, another, of a man and dog wandering passed an idyllic cottage.

Of the places I personally knew. the most instantly recognizable was Cheltenham. The large landscape of a cricket match upon the College field came with an even larger price tag. Jack seemed to cast a critical glance at it before biting his bottom lip. 'I've got an agent,' he said, as if explaining.

It's a peculiar concept, but the self-taught tend to underestimate their creative worth, especially as education gets treated like currency.

'We were a sporty family not an arty one,' said Jack. 'I was so busy playing cricket I didn't even do art at school. But, for some unknown reason, pictures and painting had always fascinated me. We were playing at Worcester where if you get two drops of rain the ground's flooded. We had two or three days of sitting twiddling our thumbs before I stormed into town and bought a sketchpad and some pencils. Call it pig-headedness or typical Russell, but I thought to myself: if Rembrandt can do it, then why can't I?

'Then I strolled along the Severn at the back of the ground. But I was so shy that whenever someone came along, I'd hide the pad.'

His mood became contemplative 'Cricket can get quite hectic. It's hard work,' he continued. 'That's why I love doing it. It's a challenge. But it's nice to split it up with the painting. I never imagined that I could make a living from art. It was strictly a hobby to fill in time. Life's too short as it is, and I don't like to waste a single moment of a single day.'

Wise chapper, I thought. His works, undoubted things of beauty, were clearly balm to his soul. He had turned the elusive secret of the wicketkeeper's art, that of simultaneous concentration and relaxation, into the art of brush and palette.

Jack confirmed this. 'From the mental side of things it's nice to be sat in a field on your own in the middle of nowhere, peace and quiet listening to the birds and that very therapeutic for me, I think. And it helps balance up with the cricket so when I go back on the cricket field hopefully I'm recharged mentally and fire up and ready to go.'

And for him to use the words 'fire up' was very much in keeping with his keen interest in military history. The heroics of Waterloo or Trafalgar or such edifying feats of Napoleonic bravery could be as inspirational to him as a picturesque landscape. Indeed, commissions have come his way from august institutions like the Imperial War Museum. But again, there's a time and place for everything.

Angus Fraser described Jack's corner of the dressing-room as 'resembling the front of a charity shop on a Monday morning'. Jack, however, knew exactly where things were. His kit bag would contain little plastic boxes full of sewing equipment and pimpled rubber so that he could repair any piece of gear, and under his chair he stuffed cereal boxes, tea bags and biscuits.

Of the people who had known Jack, Peter West probably held strong opinion in the halls of comparison. 'Jack Russell has to be up there with the very best,' he pontificated. 'I'm inclined to think, Leslie Ames was my schoolboy hero, back in the mists of time. He was a wonderful batsman, and had one or two hundreds which wasn't bad for a county wicketkeeper. He batted at number seven for England which shows how strong England batting was in those days.

'Then there was Godfrey Evans. On his day I've never seen anybody better. But for day in day out, I think, probably Alan Knott, again of Kent, was greatest. My old county always seems to produce wicketkeepers. Knotty was more consistent than Godfrey, though Godfrey rose to the big occasion.

'Bob Taylor, was a beautiful wicketkeeper. Jack Russell? A beautiful wicketkeeper of the very highest class.'

And it's sad since Ian Botham retired England hadn't managed to find a bowling-batting all rounder quite good enough at either specialty. Back in the recent past the selectors thought they needed six batsmen and five bowlers, so poor old Jack was left out despite the fact that his Test average was pretty near a respectable 30.

On debut Jack made a half century, scoring 94 against Sri Lanka at Lords in 1988. The achievement galvanized John Etheridge of the *Sun* to headline above a photo of a leaping, helmeted Jack, gripping his bat held by its blade: 'CRACKER'. John's column continued the exultation after Jack had got out. 'They rose to their feet once more, all 28,000 at Lord's to hail one of cricket's greatest and most loved eccentrics. For the second day running, the famous ground accorded a standing ovation to the quirky character.' And no one would have clapped harder than Jack's Shire and England team-mate David Lawrence, whose three wickets in the match further assisted the home side to a 7 wicket win.

Many are adamant Jack remained the best wicketkeeper in the kingdom even after he announced his retirement from the international game in the autumn of 1998. Jack hadn't found the pressure of playing for England hard to cope with, instead, according to Mike Atherton, it was the pressure he placed upon himself in trying to live up to his idol, Allan Knott, and trying for perfection every time he walked on to the park. 'Perfection,' wrote Atherton, 'is a laudable aim in sport but rarely, if ever, is it attainable.

Then as now cricket can be a perverse game. Courtney Walsh played with distinction for a decade and ended his days in Bristol without so much as a pot to wash. On the other hand Ian Harvey helped the county win five cups in five years of otherwise modest attainment. And Kim Barnett, who spent twenty years at Derby before bailing out to join to the Shire, must have felt that he's been sprinkled with fairy dust. The wand, though, belonged to the batty man with the gloves.

Like Bomber Wells before him, Jack loved a cuppa. More so, perhaps. A much dunked and squidged teabag hung from a nail during its owner's reign as England's Test match keeper. In his tea-drinking pomp Jack would get through twenty cups a day. He used to dip the tea bag in once, add plenty of milk, before hanging the bag up ready for subsequent use. In the final Test against Australia at the Oval in 1989 he used the same bag for all five days, which roughly equates to a hundred cups, each more anaemic than the last.

Lunch was two Weetabix. These had to be soaked for precisely eight minutes so that their consistency was soft, not mushy. He could tell when they had only been in for five minutes. And on those occasions the 12th man got a rollocking.

And for seconds - a mashed banana. Mostly, his team-mates humoured him.

In the summer of 2008 Mark Alleyne, Gloucestershire's head coach since 2005, parted company with the county. Mark's departure must surely have been keenly felt by Jack, if for no other reason than Boo Boo having once stumped Ritchie Richardson off a gentle off-spinning delivery, to make the former Windies captain Jack's primary first-class bowling wicket. 'The smartest stumping I've ever seen,' remarked Jack.

Ritchie was left bemused, and not for the first time. For he'd been the chap who while playing village cricket in Zum had mistaken the sting of nettles for the bites of snakes.

As for Jack, he rejoined the Shire as 'team mentor', which, reading between the lines, meant 'father figure' and tea-time baked beans. 'Russell will be responsible for off-the-field guidance, an eyes and ears and moral support for Jon Lewis,' announced a club spokesman.

A member of the Jessop Taverners claims to have genuflected, anxious about certain aspects of the paternal influence.

Jon as club skipper felt the need to express his own feelings. 'Jack has been inspirational to me, and the team. It can only be a good thing to have him back within the dressing-room.' And God help the dressing-room, was the sentiment of some other bods. Anyway, it was an interim post while Gloucestershire courted John Bracewell to return for 2009. Which, he did.

I once asked Jack if he'd ever considered living away from the Shire, somewhere like say, Zum. He looked at me as if I was potty. His reply was heartfelt.

'I was born in Stroud and followed the county from a small age. Why play for anybody else except your home county?' he said. 'A lot of the landscapes in my paintings are Gloucestershire landscapes. I do love the place very much. And hopefully I'll be around the place for the rest of my life. '

So it was with some alarm, a short while ago, that I noticed a tweet from Sybil Ruscoe. 'If you're in the Malverns pls look out for missing Jack Russell'.

Thankfully, a couple of hours later Sybil tweeted again. 'Relief – it looks like Stan the missing Jack Russell has been found 35 miles away in Stroud.' Well, that's somehow appropriate, I thought.

Listening to the brass band beside the cricket pitch in Corfu Town I made a suggestion to Gareth and Chris. 'What if we poddle back to Ano Perithia?' My wife looked at me suspiciously.

'Yes,' I said, 'I could scrawl "R.C. Russell, Stroud" somewhere amongst the graffiti on the schoolroom walls. It might raise comment one day.'

Chris giggled impishly. 'I'll happily to spread the word. The legend of Jack could become as famous here as the likes of Lear.'

No nonsense. Given Corfu's patron saint Spiridion had his mummified corpse lying in a church just along the street from where we stood, and what with the Flowerpot man stating a desire that his hands be amputated after his death and preserved in formaldehyde, Chris might unwittingly have been hitting near the truth.

Pondering on a teetotaller pickled, I chose to ignore Gareth muttering under his breath something about his 'Sainted Aunt'.

Jack Russell: The CV

Born:	August 15th 1963, Stroud, Gloucestershire.
First-class career:	1981-2004, 465 matches. Left-handed batsman, off-break bowler and wicketkeeper. He became the youngest Gloucestershire wicketkeeper (17 years, 307 days) on debut in 1981. Made eight dismissals - a record for a 'keeper on first-class debut'. Set world record of 11 catches in a match against S Africa at Johannesburg in 1995.
Tests:	Debut versus Sri Lanka, 1988; final Test versus W. Indies, 1998. In 54 Tests, He held 153 catches and made 12 stumpings.
ODIs:	Made 40 appearances, 41 catches, six stumpings.
Coaching:	Gloucestershire 'team mentor', 2008.

'A quiet man's tea is soon gone.'
Irish Proverb.

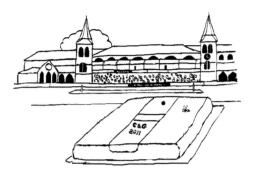

Howzat Pudding and Ballroom

'Life is a festival only to the wise.'
Ralph Waldo.

By its very nature a rarity isn't commonplace, so it was odd two should come together.

Towards the end of July contenders for promotion from Division 2 of the County Championship were beginning to sort themselves out. And at Cheltenham's co-ed establishment of quality, where Shire played Surrey on the College lawns, it was T-shirt weather.

Here, an aeon ago, with the idyllic Cotswold Hills, and the soft-stoned Gothic Victorian grandeur of the Chapel, as his stage backdrop, the Big 'Un took 17 Nottinghamshire wickets in a match, 7 of them in the course of 17 balls, without conceding a run.

Trolling up as I eventually did at 2.30 on a Saturday afternoon in 2011, ticket sales were slow. Strange, I thought. Things were set up nicely for another exciting finish.

A week ago the Shire had won at Cheltenham in the County Championship for the first time in ten years, just before tea on the third day. A sorry looking Kent had been well and truly turned over.

'Tales' aka Chris Taylor, had batted introspectively through the second day to emerge as the Shire hero. By a single reverse sweep he demonstrated hidden extrovert depths. The sole team survivor from the 2001 Cheltenham win that had seen him make a century against Sussex, he drove beautifully, and defended properly, getting himself into line. His cuts, too, were impeccable, with the exception of a late one. This emerged from the gloom to cannon off the surprised face of Martin van Jaarsveld. As slip catches go, it was technically a chance – one more about ending up in A&E than grabbing the cherry.

Generally, however, Kent's bowling was nurdled around with ease, and the scoring rate was high, even for Cheltenham. The rate was aided and abetted by the Antiguan born quickie Robbie Joseph sending down 16 no-balls. Not once did he appear to reevaluate his run-up. Instead, it was left to the Shire to show discipline. And so they did, until Captain Giddo blotted his copybook swiping across the line at a rare straight one from Robbie, falling ell bee, far short of a big score that was there for the taking. Yet, by the close of play on that second day, the chatter in the pubs of the Shire was about whether Tales could score his first career double hundred. On 192, he was poised to do so. His previous best was 196, scored against Nottinghamshire, again in 2001.

It was not to be.

Tales clipped the first ball of the final day bowled by David Balcombe, on loan from Hampshire, crisply to the cover boundary; the second, he edged behind to that notable son of Kundiawa, Papua New Guinea, wicky Geraint Jones. The anguish felt around the ground was palpable. Tales simply hung his head, and trudged off slower than an arthritic sloth. Gawd, 196, again.

But the crowd's chagrin was soon dispelled after the hosts were finally dismissed for 515. Kamikaze Kent crumbled in their second innings. And the coup de gras was delivered without anaesthetic. Number 11, Robbie Joseph, had only blessed the crease for a minute before David Payne had one thump into the pads. Umpire Martin Bodenham raised his finger.

Cheltenham College erupted in the fashion normally reserved for one-day shenanigans. David wheeled away, to be mobbed by a leaping, dancing scrum of his teammates. All save one. Alone at first slip, Captain Giddo raised both his arms in understated celebratory relief. Then, some bod shoved a pint of beer into his hand, and he too was submerged amongst a jolly gaggle of players and spectators that eventually meandered off to Montpellier Wine Bar marquee.

As for Kent, they hadn't been beaten at Cheltenham for over half a century. In 1956 the likes of Phebey, Cowdrey, Evans and Fagg lost by an innings and 75 runs to a Shire that incorporated Milton, Graveney, Wells and Crapp. The Kamikaze boys never recovered from a miserable first innings total of 45, losing 9 wickets for 20. The slow arms of Bomber Wells and Cecil 'Sam' Cook shared the haul.

Against Captain Giddo's troops, however, the defeat had been worse - an innings and 142 runs. For Giddo the spirit of day had had added pleasures. 'We used to come to the Festival as kids with our old man, and he was watching. College success was special for us all, Dad included. Performance-wise, it was probably our best executed performance of the season.'

And now for Surrey, I thought.

In the white canvas tentlet guarding the school lawns ad hoc entry point, a trio of pensionable gatemen had lost themselves to a game of cards. One of their number, wearing a white cap a tad askew, looked up sympathetically from his palpably weak hand as I spoke of queuing caravans on the M5.

To be fair, lassitude, more than motorway shuffling, meant I'd missed the morning session of Day 4. This was slightly embarrassing when one considers the tenacious Billy Midwinter. The first mainstream trans-oceanic commuter, he was only cricketer to have played for Australia when they took on England, and for England when they reciprocated.

Born in St Briavels in the Forest of Dean, the son of a miner pater keen to swap coal for gold, Billy emigrated to Oz as a babe in arms. Having honed his all-round cricketing skills, Billy took 5 for 28 for Australia in England's first innings of the famous 1877 Test match.

The sharp-eyed Big 'Un noted Billy's birthplace qualified him for the Shire. A word was said in Billy's ear, and he became one of the county's first regular professionals. In a thirty-six month period from 1880 to 1882 he played six full seasons, three in Australia, mainly for Victoria, and three in England, chiefly for the Shire. During this time he spent the equivalent of a year aboard ships. Against this, English motorways pale into insignificance.

The capped gateman relieved me of a tenner before saying, 'You come to say goodbye to JJ, then? Did you know 'is number 18 shirt's being retired? Out of respect for his services over the years, so to speak. No Gloucester player'll ever wear the number again.'

My M5 dawdling had deprived me of heart-breaking news. England's perennial twelfth man, veteran Jon Lewis had announced he was leaving the Shire after 16 seasons. What wouldn't be missed was the legendary tuttle of pongy boots that forever had spilled from his Nevil Road changing room locker.

The sensational start he'd made to his belated international call up seemed like yesterday. In a Twenty20 game against Australia in 2005, the year before being appointed Shire captain, he took four prize wickets - Ponting, Symonds, Clarke and Martyn - as the visitors were skittled out for 79 leaving England victors by 100 runs. JJ finished with four for 24 in four overs.

And with over 4900 runs, and over a 1000 wickets to boast of in first-class and one-day cricket for the Shire, where was he headed? Ironically, given the opposition at Cheltenham that day, Surrey.

'Bloomin' 'eck,' I said, 'S'pose he's fully acquainting himself.'

I decided to put thoughts of cats amongst pigeons behind me. Beyond the card-playing tableau, I joined 1500 diehards, the lowest attendance of the festival. Obviously, a Shire victory wasn't generally anticipated. Needing another 130 to win Surrey were only one down, and the obdurate Mark 'The Hips' Ramprakash, a first innings centurion, was at the crease.

A languidly flapping seagull, as gurt as a four-legged Jack Russell, cruised by the press full balcony of the twin spired pavilion. The bird seemed to provide a distraction from a worrying torpor out in the middle. Its quick, low 'qua-qua-qua,' was the closest thing to a duck evidenced over the previous three days, and the gull drew the attention of a smattering of aged punters

'Whur's 'e cum from?' some codger questioned.

'Same place as rest of them greedy buggers, Glawster Daarks,' his neighbour confidently asserted.

Daarks? Oh, 'Docks', of course. The yelping clamour of disgust overhead made it obvious the feathered visitor had a gang of followers, more like citygulls than seagulls, which had, by now, appeared to fascinate Umpire Llong and several Shire fielders.

The gulls were too late, however. The hospitality tents and bins offered thin pickings. Such is twenty-hours. The day before had been very different. As Chris Dent raised his bat celebrating his match 100, several dozen women, dressed to impress, 'gathered for nibbles'. These, along with the traditional Howzat Pudding, a chocolate cake shaped like a cricket pitch, the centerpiece of 'Ladies Day', were history.

The former Dynasty actress, Willesden's Emma Samms had teetered on her heels to present the sweet pud to the Shire Chairman Rex Body.

Perhaps, a former chap in the post, John Light, would have relished annual helpings of Howzat Pudding. Who's to say. But certainly he personifies the Cotswold trait of independent spirit, and believes nowhere sums up the area better than the Cheltenham Cricket Festival. And this is where one will find him absorbing the view from the boundary. Having all of Gloucestershire there, Leckhampton Hill, Cleeve Hill, the buildings of the college, and the crowd, moves him 'to tears.'

He's been coming since 1949. The Shire were playing Surrey, and the first ball he saw bowled was by Jim Laker. Then McIntyre, the Surrey keeper, stumped Jack Crapp. But the wicket had been broken so quickly, John thought Jack was bowled.

Poignantly, when his father was dying in Gloucester Hospital, John said to him, 'Remember the first ball I saw at Cheltenham - Laker bowled Crapp'. His father said, 'No, he didn't; McIntyre stumped him.'

'I didn't believe it,' John recently revealed. 'But I came home and looked it up in Wisden, and my father was right. It had happened so quickly that, as a little boy, I didn't realise.'

And, 'Howzaaaat!' was the sudden collective scream from the middle as I looked on. JJ had welcomed his first acquaintance of the afternoon – the edge of Hamilton-Brown's bat.

'If you're going to flash, flash in front of the ladies!' an anonymous wag yelled.

He drew a loud response. 'Impossible! They were 'ere YESTERDAY!' Cue healthy round of applause.

Goody, goody, the atmosphere was improving. And before I could recite Grace at Gloucester two more wickets followed. The Shire were in the game.

Ramprakash, though, continued to effortlessly nurdle, oblivious to a stinging attack from near the now busy scoreboard. Among stalls of hog roast, fish 'n' chips, and waffles offering death by coronary, that of Pedigree 'the official beer of England' presented demise by wasp.

One such creature, showing its tenacity, had targeted a slowly retreating tray of full pints. Flicked at by the bare-chested carrier, the wasp responded by impaling itself in the unfortunate's exposed torso. Both a slight wobble and a frothy spillage were discernable. As was the grimace of pain, and the beseeching baritone of 'Someone, PLEASE take this pissing tray off me. NOW!'

An unattended open-sided tent gave me sensible sanctuary. Curiously, on close inspection, the inside held a long trestle table loaded with motley cricket books. And someone had given pride of place to a mint condition display of Mike Vockins' biography Arthur Milton - Last of the Double Internationals.

All the other books were second hand, and well thumbed. My own digit added more patina to a signed copy of Jack Russell's autobiography, a tatty eight quid booklet on Proctor, and assorted eighteen quid knackered biographies of WG Grace and Tom Graveney.

Zum, too, had a presence. And, as I went from perusing a 1970s testimonial programme of Hallam Moseley to a signed one of Derek Taylor, I sensed being watched.

A thin nobbly-kneed bloke in a bushwacker safari hat and canvas shorts broke off over-the-boundary-board chit-chat with Captain Giddo's wicket taking little brother, Will, and rose from his picnic chair. Perhaps they'd been debating when two pairs of brothers had played in the same team before. Maybe, the Gidmans and the Taylors were the first.

Looking as if he'd taken wrong turn in the Serengeti, the bushwacker buckled a money pouch around his waist as he strode purposefully across to where I browsed.

He had sniffed a sale.

Feeling obliged, I selected a fusty yellowed paperback and dug for small change.

On realizing he'd encountered my sort on many an occasion, he confided matter-of-factly. 'Books on Gloucestershire cricket don't sell. I sell books at county grounds from Worcester to Canterbury, but there's never any demand for Gloucester.'

Surely, I hoped, there must be exceptions. He must have read my thoughts.

He tapped an Arthur Milton. 'Mind you, I've sold 38 of these over the Festival. Have you got an interest?'

'Indirectly,' I said. A more sensible chap than I, called Louis Untermeyer, once advised: 'Write out of love. Write out of instinct. Write out of reason. But always for money.'

However, sometimes there's no going back.

My eyes took in the empty plastic chairs, marquees and gazebos. Two ladies sat together. One, her blonde dyed hair showing brown roots, had a sunburnt right arm and a pale left one. Perhaps, she too had been stuck on the motorway. She sipped orange juice as her friend read a Kindle, a snoozing Pug at their feet. A pensioner immersed himself writing neatly in a large scorebook, while, close by, a chap stroked the ears of a Labrador. Another bloke, I guessed to be in his 40s, sat back satisfied having successfully perched a collapsible Sheriff Woody toy on a boundary board, allowing it to watch the match. And just in the nick of time.

Ramprakash, in navigational difficulty, had bizarrely contrived to get himself out, 'obstructing the field'.

Peter West having taking to puffing at his ubiquitous pipe beside the angels, and experienced in having presented the predecessor of *Strictly Come Dancing, Come Dancing,* on BBC television for many years, would have reluctantly awarded the 2006 *Strictly* winner low marks. For, in the spontaneous opinion of umpire George Sharp, 'Ramps' quick step wasn't in the spirit of 'ballroom.'

Ramps was adjudged to have impeded Ian Saxelby as the Shire player went to gather Kane Williamson's throw at the bowler's end as Jason Roy went for a risky second run. The Shire's fielders looked frustrated more than anything else, but Ramps was a long way off the pitch. That's to say, three pitches across. A harsh decision. Certainly Ramps thought so. He started walking off but returned to talk to umpires George Sharp and Nigel Llong before eventually departing.

At 137 for 4 Surrey had been cruising. No longer. Zafar Ansari, in after Ramps, was out for a proper duck, a golden one, ell bee to a JJ pad rapper. After that it was nip and tuck until Surrey sneaked home by two wickets. Victory for them was a close run thing.

Making my way back to the car, I cast a glance at my 35p book purchase *Moments in Cricket.* That afternoon it had become further out of date.

GLOUCESTERSHIRE v KENT

LV County Championship 2011 (Division 2)
Venue: College Ground, Cheltenham on
20th, 21st, 22nd July 2011 (4-day match)
Toss: Gloucestershire won the toss and decided to field
Points: Gloucestershire 24 (Batting 5, Bowling 3); Kent 3 (Batting 1, Bowling 2)
Umpires: MJD Bodenham, MA Gough

Kent first innings

JL Denly		b Lewis	13
CD Piesley	lbw	b Lewis	0
SA Northeast	c Coughtrie	b WRS Gidman	34
*M van Jaarsveld	c and b Marshall		1
DI Stevens	c Taylor	b Saxelby	67
+GO Jones	c Coughtrie	b WRS Gidman	0
AJ Blake	c Marshall	b WRS Gidman	2
JC Tredwell	c Coughtrie	b WRS Gidman	45
SJ Cook	c Dent	b WRS Gidman	6
DJ Balcombe	c WRS Gidman	b Saxelby	12
RH Joseph	not out		8
Extras (4 b, 6 lb, 4 nb, 3 w)			17
Total (all out, 63.3 overs)			205

Fall of wickets:
1-1 (Piesley, 3 ov), 2-21 (Denly, 6.5 ov), 3-43 (van Jaarsveld, 12.2 ov), 4-55 (North-east, 13.5 ov), 5-55 (Jones, 15.2 ov), 6-59 (Blake, 17.4 ov), 7-142 (Tredwell, 47.3 ov), 8-154 (Cook, 51.4 ov), 9-180 (Balcombe, 55.5 ov), 10-205 (Stevens, 63.3 ov)

Gloucestershire bowling	Overs	Mdns	Runs	Wkts
Lewis	16	4	49	2
Saxelby	13.3	2	49	2
Payne	14	3	51	0
Marshall	6	2	8	1
WRS Gidman	14	4	38	5

Gloucestershire first innings

CDJ Dent	c Jones	b Stevens	12
HJH Marshall		b Tredwell	37
KS Williamson	c Jones	b Balcombe	29
DA Payne	c van Jaarsveld	b Balcombe	14
CG Taylor	c Jones	b Balcombe	196
*APR Gidman	lbw	b Joseph	79
IA Cockbain	c and b Balcombe		19
WRS Gidman	c van Jaarsveld	b Tredwell	5
+RG Coughtrie	c Jones	b Stevens	18
J Lewis	c van Jaarsveld	b Balcombe	14
ID Saxelby	not out		6
Extras (2 b, 10 lb, 42 nb, 2 w)			56
Total (all out, 118.2 overs)			515

Fall of wickets:
1-13 (Dent, 7.5 ov), 2-91 (Marshall, 25.1 ov), 3-97 (Williamson, 28.3 ov), 4-116 (Payne, 33 ov), 5-276 (APR Gidman, 68.1 ov), 6-353 (Cockbain, 82.4 ov), 7-444 (WRS Gidman, 97.5 ov), 8-490 (Taylor, 112.2 ov), 9-506 (Coughtrie, 115.5 ov), 10-515 (Lewis, 118.2 ov)

Kent bowling	Overs	Mdns	Runs	Wkts
Balcombe	29.2	5	103	5
Stevens	20	7	68	2
Joseph	19	0	110	1
Cook	17	0	87	0
Tredwell	29	3	118	2
Denly	4	0	17	0

Kent second innings

JL Denly	lbw	b Saxelby	26
CD Piesley		b Payne	4
SA Northeast	c Coughtrie	b Payne	0

*M van Jaarsveld	lbw	b Lewis	12
DI Stevens	c Coughtrie	b Lewis	35
+GO Jones	lbw	b Lewis	20
AJ Blake	run out		9
JC Tredwell	c and b Williamson		5
SJ Cook	not out		46
DJ Balcombe	c Saxelby	b Payne	1
RH Joseph	lbw	b Payne	0
Extras (1 b, 3 lb, 6 w)			10
Total (all out, 42.5 overs)			168

Fall of wickets:
1-24 (Piesley, 8.3 ov), 2-24 (Northeast, 9 ov), 3-32 (Denly, 9.5 ov), 4-67 (van Jaarsveld, 21.2 ov), 5-102 (Jones, 27.1 ov), 6-106 (Stevens, 29.3 ov), 7-119 (Tredwell, 32.1 ov), 8-151 (Blake, 38.3 ov), 9-168 (Balcombe, 42.3 ov), 10-168 (Joseph, 42.5 ov)

Gloucestershire bowling	Overs	Mdns	Runs	Wkts
Lewis	12	2	31	3
Saxelby	8	2	26	1
Payne	11.5	1	60	4
WRS Gidman	6	1	16	0
Williamson	5	0	31	1

Gloucestershire won by an innings and 142 runs

Tail End Wagging

FIFTEEN

Of Nicks and Gipsy Bones

'Cricket is stressful, nerve-wracking, and mentally and
physically exhausting, but it is always a 'pleasure'.'

Cheltenham College Prospectus.

Sometimes one can't see the willow for the ancient beech wood. This is the case at Cranham, secreted away in a steep-sided Cotswold valley. The village cricket club cut and chased its first leather upon the Knoll in 1887. Understandably, the club badge portrays a leafy tree. A tad more perplexing is the added depiction of a heron. Possibly this is just be a gentle nudge. The club batters have the occasional habit of fishing outside the off stump.

Should the heron prove too subtle, out of sight between the wooden slated pavilion and a couple of shabby wooden sheds much in need of TLC or demolition storing the groundsman's gubbins is an improvised practice area. Here a metal beer barrel serves as an improvised wicket. Behind it, the glass panes of an inviting pavilion window offer more of a deterrent than any slip carefully placed for that nick off the outside edge.

One might be forgiven in thinking that Cranham's team was somewhat makeshift. 'Ancient Mariner' wore the wicky's cymbals , 'The Horse' was quickish, 'Pig' slow, and this being the Laurie Lee country, the Captain was, understandably, 'Rosie', although really it's A. Pockett. Bryony, the real girl in the team, was one of a couple of Overs.

Adding furthers local confusion is pop singer cum songwriter Lily Allen. She of the explicit song lyric lives close by in a three million spondoolick country pile. Her song 22, however, is definitely not about the twenty-two yards of Cranham's cricket pitch.

Nor is 'Gladys Leap' a collective term for the Shire's Gladiators behaving in the manner of lemmings, despite a seasonal tendency for diving at the end of suicidal runs. It was a short cut, one to save a rather longer walk than the one back to the pavilion.

Gladys was actually Gladys Hillier an inspiring Cranham postwoman who used to leap the three feet across a local brook on her round to save herself a couple of miles. Indeed, during the time when cricketing chartered accountant, and former Chairman of England selectors, David Graveney was Shire captain, folk rockers Fairport Convention were so charmed by Gladys' story that they named their mid '80s album *Glady's Leap* in her honour. Even the Ordnance Survey has recognized her place of launch.

Now, happily for the likes of Goose and myself, the chance of pulling a muscle has diminished since the arrival of a footbridge. And accompanied by a small wicker basket, we crossed its little span as Shire cricket snoozed apart from Autumn renovations, spiking, scarifying, top dressing and spraying.

Our intent was to fungi forage in Saltridge Common Woods betwixt and between Cranham and Sheepscombe. Stroud was a mile or so away along the A46, and its traffic was an audible faint hum. Mist steamed. This my light spirit likened to the romance of smoke from Gipsy fires. It further struck me that Cranham had entertained Gloucestershire Gipsies not long ago, maybe on account of it being perceived by those particular gipsies as 'a better club', given that, in early fixtures certainly, they would only condescend to play against these, or major schools in the county.

Should further clarification be needed, Gloucestershire Gipsies are of a wandering persuasion only when it comes to cricket. They promote a good spirit of amateurism without recourse to horses, canary-coloured caravans, tinkering tools or bunches of lavender. And they are of the same ilk as the Devon Dumplings and the Hampshire Hogs, and the oldest, and perhaps most illustrious of them all, I Zingari, named after the Italian for 'gipsies'. Zum's President Sir Spencer Ponsonby-Fane had coined that name for his elite bunch of itinerants way back in 1845.

It wasn't until September 1921 that six gentlemen met in Bristol to discuss the possible formation of a County Amateur Cricket Club in the Shire. Rather than also trying to be clever in adopting 'Gitanos', 'Zigeuners', or 'Ciganos', plumping for 'Gipsies' kept things plain and simple. Four months later, during the 1st General meeting at Gloucester's Bell Hotel, it was agreed that there should be three principal qualification rules regarding membership:

> *'Birth or permanent residence in the county with the county being divided into geographical divisions, each of which should be represented on the committee.'*

'Cricketers should also be, at the same time, acceptable guests in the average country-house.'

and,

'The club colours should be old gold and maroon, the very same colours as depicted in the Arms of the County.'

Sorry to say, in the early days the membership was a tad snobby. Favouritism was towards public schools and the military, so no oiks. In the 1960s, one prospective new member was turned down quite flatly. The reasons? He attended Cheltenham Grammar School rather than Cheltenham College, and only had one initial.

Of those that did tick the right boxes Cyril Hollinshead was the most enduring. The Big 'Un was 54 and still scoring first-class centuries in the year Cyril was born. Yet, it was just before the outbreak of Second World War that Cyril turned his left arm over for the Gipsies for the first time. Fast in his day, he embarked on a life in which a love for cricket bordered on addiction. War must have come as a considerable inconvenience. Within twelve months of the cessation of hostilities Cyril had made a first-class appearance for the Shire. But that game against Cambridge University was his one and only as Shire opportunities went. On the up side, he could to turn his full attention to the Gipsies. And he did. Whether batting or in the field he would become a chap who gave the tortoise a sporting chance.

In 1988 a snippet emerged in the *Gloucestershire Echo*, the Cheltenham evening paper that he'd edited for 29 years until 1967:

'Over 86 And Did Not Get A Bowl.

'A treasured record went by the board when Cyril Hollinshead played his latest game of cricket – at the age of 86 years and 90 days. He turned out for Gloucestershire Gypsies against Malvern Cryptics at Malvern College and complained: "Do you know, it was the first time in 49 years of playing for the Gipsies, that I didn't bowl?"

'He also did not score, because he was out second ball, but he loved playing, even if the Gipsies all out 157, did lose by eight wickets.

'"I hared after the ball two or three times from mid-off, but always saw something go past me like an express train – another fielder," he said. "But I did manage to get to the ball first once."'

Despite feeling snubbed Cyril was a stoic and persevered with his Gipsy life for another four seasons. Aged 90, he finally called it a day after being allowed a trundle in which he bowled six overs for 16 runs. Over a span that began in 1911, 81 years before its conclusion, Cyril had taken 4,000 wickets in club matches.

He 'fell asleep' on November 25, 1995, aged 93, and would perhaps have been sorry to have missed out on the Gipsies recently jetting off to St. Moritz to have a go at playing cricket on a frozen Swiss lake.

As the mist continued to steam, Goose and I continued our expedition. The bright autumnal sunshine on morning dew and a myriad of webs gave a look of early snow. Right and proper, I thought, with Gustav Holst, in 1910, composing the tune for the Christina Rossetti carol *In the Bleak Midwinter* in a Cranham cottage opposite the Black Horse Inn, where Cranham's cricketers converged to play shove-ha'penny, or to tuck into portions of Toad-in-the-Hole the size of the family Bible, or purely just to bibble.

'Well, I can only call it a crap season,' said Goose, jolting me out of my reverie.

'What, autumn?'

'No twiticus, ruddy Gloucestershire's!' His voice, raised slightly higher than I think he intended, made a blackbird chak-chak-chak its alarm and a pheasant to rise airborne with a loud clatter.

'Goodness sake, keep your voice down, the woods have ears,' I said in a hushed tone.

Goose bent down and picked a 'penny bun', one of those robust fungi that foodies call a 'cep', and crave as an accompaniment to saddle of rabbit. 'Funny, the name hasn't changed with the times to keep in line with the weighty rise of professional cricketers wages.'

Holding the cep between middle finger and thumb, Goose was either inspecting his find for unwanted maggots, or imagining himself preparing to bowl a top-spinner. 'I mean look at the likes of Hamish Marshall, and twirlyman Murali. So, Penny bun, my arse. This little fella should be inflated to the ten quid bun by now. '

'Well, at least the Shire's dragged itself into the black,' I said. 'We mustn't forget there's two-thousand quid profit, new money, in the coffers.'

'Oh, woopedy-doop! That's … ' Goose's brain began to tick. '… a mere four-hundred and six thousand less than Zum.

'Just be thankful for Cheltenham's all-time record gate receipts.'

'That doesn't necessarily mean more people.' Goose carefully placed his cep in the basket.

Of course, he was right. As with ten quid buns, so with tickets, I thought.

'I'm sure things will get better moneywise if the Gladirags could discover ways of not getting themselves out. Perhaps, they already have.' I recalled the little pots of greasy stuff I'd seen in the Shire's Nevil Road changing room a few days before the arrival of Sky's TV cameras.

If not particularly forward thinking, Reverend Holmes was, perhaps, a tad naïve. In 1893, a time of Englishmen being groomed as honest decent sorts, he wrote 'we know as much of the history of cricket as we shall ever know now, and we have been told everything relating to the science of the game. There is no fresh ground to be explored.'

He wasn't making a reference to strong coffee. Nor could one could blame the reverend for not having made a connection between cricket bats and the greasy invention, by American Robert Chesebrough twenty years earlier. Vaseline Petroleum Jelly, having its origin in the Pennsylvania Oil Fields, couldn't have been further removed from cricket. Anyway, had the link been made, to speak of negating contact friction and elevated local temperature would have been regarded among his peers as gobbledygook.

Ah ha, I thought. Had John Bracewell been listening to pertinent whispers allude to on the airwaves?

On monitor duty in the *Test Match Special* commentary box Phil Tufnell had been giving 'Hot Spot', the infra-red imaging system used to determine whether the ball had nicked the bat, his close scrutiny.

'Let's have a look at the replays. Bat's nowhere near the pad, and there looks to be a clear, if tiny, deviation as ball passes pad. Nothing on Hot Spot. Third umpire Billy Bowden just will not give that.

'It's absolutely worthless. You know as a cricketer when someone has got a fine scratchy outside edge.'

Quiet rumours about smearing Vaseline on bat edges to defeat heat-seeking technology are now in vogue. However, not wanting to sound prejudiced, other petroleum-based tinctures for self-effacing batters are also available on chemist shelves. As to the pots in the Shire changing room I make no further comment.

Beside a coppice of hazel I put things in a nutshell. 'The Shire's got funky plans. The club's said as much, itself.'

Goose cast me one of his frowns. 'Let's get back to Glady's Leap. We might get lucky with the Chanterelles.'

*

History, from a time when a 'penny bun' was probably still holding its value, has shown that a nick off the outside edge doesn't necessarily mean disaster. It can also prove devastatingly effective, as an evocative match report in *The Citizen*, Wednesday July 20, 1955, reveals involving the Woodpeckers, a cricket team from Ashleworth near Gloucester and the Gloucestershire Police:

Thrilling KO Final Won In Last Over

An American film company would undoubtedly have billed it as Stupendous! Colossal! Magnificent! Even the more phlegmatic English cricket lover would refer to it as a memorable, exciting match, this Gloucestershire Knock-out Cup Final played at the Spa yesterday evening before a huge and appreciative crowd and won by gallant Woodpeckers, who beat the fading light and Gloucester Police in the very last over of the game.

When Police had taken first knock and compiled the excellent score of 124 in their allotted 20 overs only a few perhaps of the Woodpecker supporters grace their side more than an outside chance of victory.

And when Woodpeckers in their reply had lost 4 wickets with only 40 runs on the board even the hopes of heir most optimistic supporters must have dropped near zero.

But then came that superb, thrill-packed stand between Ernie Tuffley and Colin Finch that put Woodpeckers right back into the game and set the crowd alight. They thrashed the Police attack to all parts of the field and before they were separated had added a match winning 60 runs for the fifth wicket. Tuffley had hit tremendously hard for a brilliant half-century without clearing the boundary, but Finch made amends with two glorious drives for six.

Yet even on their dismissal the game was by no means over. A vital dropped catch, cheeky singles, near run-outs, desperate fielding – all added to those unforgettable final overs before the winning hit of the edge of the bat came to end the suspense.

Not that Woodpeckers provided all the thrills! Few expected better batting than that provided by the Police in their innings – calculated to be a winning total in most circumstances. They started off at a cracking pace and, except for a temporary easing of the tempo mid-way through, maintained that rate of scoring.

PC Mike Morris, PC Ken Barker, the skipper, Insp. Bob Mayo and even tail-enders Sgt. Vic Bullock and PC Ray Llewellyn executed a number of classic shots that had wrist-work as well as power, while the inimitable PC Harry Cribble contributed runs as perhaps only he can, his knock including a six and a four before he played on to the persistent Wilkes, much to the crowd's disappointment.

In the tense atmosphere mistakes were inevitable, but both sides earned applause for their efforts in the field, even when the batsmen seemed to be in full command. There could scarcely have been a more exciting or fitting finish to the competition than this match: it was almost a pity someone had to lose!

A collection on the ground realised nearly £20.

SIXTEEN

Pelicans and Coconut Bats

'Great perils have this beauty, that they bring to light the fraternity of strangers.'
Victor Hugo (French romantic writer, 1802-1885).

The mercury level of the barometer had dropped into the minuses. Outside it was too raw to be sociable. Such dark days between West Country cricket seasons were good for one thing only – cogitating. Take the French for instance. If their aristocracy had thought to teach their tenants cricket then their chateaux would not have been burned.

One should never forget that the moment the Paris mob stormed the Bastille in 1789 with yells of 'Liberté! Égalité! Fraternité!' Bullen was bowled upon Hambledon's Halfpenny Down amid gentile shouts of 'Howzat!' Since then, cricket has allowed the humbling of poshocracy with no hard feelings. And it remains a wonderful way to glue our Commonwealth together.

With my fingers numb from sub zero cold I decided to down tools, leave my study looking like a scruffy egret's nest amid thorns of an acacia tree, and catch up with leather and willow in the sunny climes of Calypso cricket where Gloucestershire ties dally.

A 'working' holiday became my excuse to follow in the footsteps of the Marylebone Cricket Club. I mean, for Heaven's sake, the club, had set the tone for cricketing conduct in the world since the 1870s. So why not check out some pitches and report back how things were shaping up, I thought.

However, a recent connection to the Shire would be nice. And much Googling chanced upon one that, I admit, was a tad tenuous. But, for my purposes, it would have to do. I'd found an archived scorecard from 2008. And upon it, Tim Hancock's name was there in black and white. I printed the scorecard off onto a sheet of A4.

Less we forget, Tim had been the Shire's vice captain for a couple of years at the start of this century, despite being plagued by bad form, not to mention a broken hand. My uncle Tubby once described him as 'officer material'. Cricket writer Sean Beynon described Tim as 'fairly accomplished', and 'naturally aggressive', and as one who 'tries to dominate the bowling'. Unfortunately, lapses of concentration cost Tim dear. In seasons past he often got to 50, but was prone to playing a naff stroke that lead to his downfall. In the outfield he was 'tremendously committed', and a 'decent occasional bowler'.

Like W.G. Grace, Tim had deserved the right to wear the red and yellow coloured hooped cap of the MCC. It reflected sound demeanor and a sense of fair play. But the difference between the men, in fishing parlance anyway, was that of a pike to a guppy.

Part of the Shire furniture since 1991, only the most ardent and optimistic Gloucestershire fans ever called for Tim to be called into the England one-day squad. And for all those faithful to the Shire, 2005 proved a watershed filled with tears. There was just a single county Championship win all that season - at Cardiff at the beginning of May. With the tone of the match set by Chris Taylor's 1st innings knock of 176, come the morning of day 4 and chasing 119 for victory, Tim guided the Shire to their target with a fine 41 not out.

Sadly, it was down hill after that, and the season concluded with the Shire being ignominiously relegated from both Division 1 of the County Championship and Division 1 of the Totesport National League. For Tim the only personal highlight that year was to enjoy his benefit. But enough was enough. Before the start of the next season Tim retired himself from first class cricket.

Some kind soul then thought Tim was deserving of a getaway and was considered a sensible choice for a 2008 MCC touring team that included two other West Country retirees, Mike Burns and Rob Turner of Zum. The latter, incidentally, had been chosen as captain.

As it was, Tim's inclusion meant my proposed journey to St. Kitts and Nevis had purpose and would ease my conscience when I sought out servings of locally caught spiny lobster. The further distraction of sea diving pelicans would be an added bonus when keypad tapping my laptop and lubricating my throat with *Carib*.

It would all have been much less of an adventure had I merely given Tim a call at his Filton College workplace. However, to had done so would have been much less fun, and very unsporting. Better to create myself a personal challenge. Rather this than possibly being asked: 'Why the hell do you want to know?' I would have had no convincing answer to that. A reason of purely adding to a bank of cricket trivia might have impressed, but I didn't hold by breath.

Happily, my flight over the Atlantic lacked hiccups, unlike the minor one encountered by the MCC when a stewardess made a faux pas four hours out of Gatwick and four short of the St Kitts capital, Basseterre. 'Ladies and gentlemen,' she announced, 'the Captain has turned on the seat belts sign as we are preparing to descend.'

I disembarked onto dry land. Notices in Basseterre airport's arrivals hall declared that work was being carried out 'expeditiously'. This, I would later glean, meant 'on island time'.

My island time began by moseying around the 36 square miles of Nevis that had more than a passing resemblance to 'Super Mario Kart Donkey Kong Island' – a volcano (now defunct) with a race circuit around it, albeit one limited to 40mph and with many a character building pothole.

Smaller than its sister St. Kitts, Nevis had simple appeal. Local tourist board literature informed 'temporary drivers should beware of donkeys, goats and people,' in that order. Such bumpff, however, wasn't very useful for finding cricket grounds. That was something left to the initiative.

Using mine, I eventually parked my bum in a none too solid, weathered wooden stand at 'Elquemedo T Willett Park', the cricket ground named in honour of the first Nevisian cricketer of five to play for the West Indies Test team. Formally called 'Grove Park' the ground has as its backdrop the spectacular cloud enshrouded Mount Nevis. Indisputably the principal cricket field on the island, it lies on the edge of the grey stone built capital Charlestown, which, although on a par with my home village in terms of population, is locally lauded as 'Queen City'.

Shaded from the heat by a tree hung with brown pods the size of cricket balls, I looked around for somebody who might give me some exaggerated local tale of Nevis v MCC derring-do, but there was nobody at close hand. A pair of brown doves eyed me cautiously. And out towards the middle of the playing area a sit-on mower motored up and down, up and down, pausing once for its grey-bearded driver, sporting dreadlocks under a multi-coloured teacosy hat, to give me a friendly wave before revving away to continue his smartening up of the outfield.

Well, this was the spot Nevis routed the MCC by 4 wickets in a game reduced by tropical sog. Despite Tim Hancock top scoring a gritty 57, Mike Burns 27 and Rob Turner 24 they all got out when seeming set, and the visitors were bowled out for not a lot inside 39 overs. According to the match report 'the fastest outfielder on display had feathers' and the home side 'simply flew out of the starting blocks and smashed the MCC bowling to all parts' reaching their target with half their overs in hand.

The probable inspiration for that editorial suddenly turned up at my feet. A road-runner of a chicken had arrived to scratch in the dust around discarded peanut shells and *Carib* bottle tops.

Beyond the ground, and more incongruous to an image of island paradise, were the vast numbers of cars that lay where they'd died - in front gardens and in the backs, on every available patch of waste ground, and on the sides of streets. Vine entangled, they were of all sizes and makes. Many had the flowers of poinciana poking their heads prettily out of rust holes. 'They're useful, man. People help themselves to bits,' Akimaba, a young entrepreneur, said after stopping his American SUV to be sociable. 'They keep 'working' cars going. And seat foam makes great cricket padding.'

For several days, with amiable strangers like Akimba, I took random long shots with the scorecard that led nowhere. Nobody though could remember anything about the match. To help me decide where to go next, the A4 now a crumple in my pocket, I went to take in the local panorama from a small, church topped, roadside hill. It was a Sunday.

Quite literally, I bumped into Samuel Tyson. A clean-shaven retired West Indian gentleman, he was immaculate in collar and tie and grey Sunday best suit. In the midday glare of Caribbean sunlight we had come from different directions to inadvertently collide at the church corner. Hasty mutual apology was followed by our self-introductions.

It didn't take me long to realize that Samuel, had 'the knowledge'.

A former GPO engineer he had decided to return to the island of his birth, 'running away from fiddly optic fibres' that were barely visible upon palm of hand. Not only had Samuel worked most of his life in England, he had also played most of his cricket there. His hero remains the Barbadian John Shepherd for no better reason that I could fathom than John being 'a lovely kind man'. Named as President of Kent in 2011 John gave eight seasons of yeoman service to the Shire during the 1980s before becoming a coach there.

Samuel's own memories of the Shire were dear.

'I played at Stone long ago and hit a ball 'boom' right into the little wooden pavil-ion,' he chuckled. 'The cherry went right through the door and rattled around a few teacups. Inside there was barely enough room for the umps to change, let alone us teams. My young son shouted at me from the boundary "Daddy, that wasn't six that was twelve!"'

'That pavilion's gone now,' I remarked. 'I wondered who knackered it.' Noticing his askance look, I hurriedly added: 'it's all new facilities at Stone now. People power. The ground attracts the great and the good of Gloucestershire cricket - Mark Alleyne, Ian Harvey, Matt Windows, you name them. You must have been the vanguard, Samuel.'

Pulling out my piece of paper I pointed at Tim Hancock's name. 'This one,' I said, 'He had his benefit match at Stone. And, of course, the offspring of one your cricketing legends also played there. Carl Greenidge? The son of Gordon?'

Carl had joined the Shire at the beginning of the fateful 2005 season. It was not a case of father like son. Whereas his dad's talent was with the willow, Carl made his name as a bowler. This is partly explained by having the legendary fast bowler Andy Roberts as a cousin on his mum's side. The Shire's head coach was Mark Alleyne. He welcomed the signing. 'I am looking forward to Carl joining what is already a successful bowling unit,' he said, 'one that can help us maintain the momentum which we have built up over the years.' That, to be fair, was bit of an unwitting faux pas.

I mean crikey, Shire supporters don't like being reminded of the last over of the 2007 T20 final shenanigans at Edgbaston. Carl, sporting a natty blue and yellow headband, was asked by Jon Lewis to bowl it. Carl decided to mix things up with short and long run-ups. In the end he only mixed himself up. Kent needed 13 to win a Nevis sized mountain it could be said. They achieved it. Darren Stevens bludgeoned a boundary off an unfortunate short-pitched over-stepping no ball. Kent were home with two deliveries spare.

Casting a glance at Samuel I noticed all of a sudden he'd become misty-eyed, losing all interest in my sheet of paper. 'Gordon Greenidge! Phew. I know him, man! Him and Vivian Richards. These islands are a small place. Both them fellows could whack it to the seagulls, but Gordon ... well, you know, he was *most* dangerous when he was limping.

'My wife and I were there for the fun of the 1984 'Blackwash' series. We had a big bag of fried chicken with us we joined the queue outside Lords at 6 o'clock in the morning for the final day of the second Test. Gordon hit 214 not out. He smote the ball as sweet as demerara cane sugar off Ian Botham's bowling. The Windies chased 342 for victory. It was glorious. I remember women coming into the ground during their lunch break and dancing in the stands. People all around me blew conch shells. And the drum music changed cricket forever.'

'Not as much as fancy dress,' I said to myself.

'And we won with only Desmond Haynes getting himself out. 344 for 1! Tell me if I'm wrong, but I think it's still the highest ever run chase at Lords.'

I could only shrug ignorance and say that Gordon had also played for the auld enemy Scotland, flippantly suggesting Golden eagles risked becoming even greater endangered.

Samuel confessed that he'd once been encouraged to turn pro. 'My turning professional was suggested by a groundsman who looked something like you,' he mused, looking me up and down. 'I always tried moving well, getting right forward and right back, but one too many balls in the wrong place and - poof.'

But for him, it was really a case of one too many bonnets. His pro dreams were shattered, together with the odd bone, when a car negligently slammed into his butt in Stoke-on-Trent. Today, he was part of the St. Kitts and Nevis cricketing community and the proud new owner of a balshy donkey given to him by his 103-year old dad to 'ride up the volcano through monkey infested rainforest'.

Another world, I thought.

Suddenly, I remembered again what I wanted to know. Samuel squinted at the page. I pointed again at Tim's name and gushed explanation. 'It's a twenty over game from March 2008. The scorecard says 'no result'. See.

'In their allotted overs St Kitts and Nevis lost 7 wickets in making 137. In reply this guy Tim Hancock hadn't made it into double figures before being out ell bee to your teenage slow left-arm Elvin Berridge. That's fair enough. But what happened next?

'The MCC lost only 6 wickets in reaching 134 in 19 overs and 5 balls and there was no result. I mean to say, did the hand of God suddenly smite down the MCC and islanders? Had a hurricane unleashed its fury before the last ball was bowled? Had the volcano surprisingly woken up? Samuel, can you shed any light on this?'

'Let me have a think for a moment...'

As he did so, I mentioned having spent a couple of days pootling about in a puny 'mash and go' automatic rental car looking at the local cricket grounds. This only served to distract Samuel once more. 'Have you got to Rambury, the pitch up behind the old slave market and primary school? That's my local pitch. As children we didn't have willow bats so we cut ours out of coconut palm trees. Even the girls would play, bowling underarm at us boys. We'd dive around after the ball getting cuts and bruises on our bare knees.'

Been to Rambury? No, I hadn't. The way there was narrow and twisty and more rut than road. But I'd been genned up thanks to a local cricket loving taxi driver.

Rambury, crapped on by grazing goats and sheep, wasn't for the faint-hearted fielder. And the outfield had more loose stones than the average mason's yard, although apparently the pitch played well and true. Amazingly, the MCC had actually won the first match of the tour there against a Nevis Under-19 side. They showed creditable character, I thought, earning many a rum punch at Charlestown highlight - Eddie's Bar.

But to be honest, being as it was off the beaten track, thoughts of Rambury had fuelled my angst after reading a local newspaper piece about a recent gang murder occurring on Samuel's 'paradisiacal' island. It was an issue I cautiously raised.

'Oh, some of our youngsters have become very naughty,' Samuel reckoned. 'They're greedy for easy money. Even cricket's become infected. There was a time not long ago when putting on the West Indies cap was enough to give a young man enormous pride. Now it's all about money. I blame that Stamford fellow. More dollars than cents.'

Or perhaps he meant 'sense'.

I wondered whether the sentiments of former Shire stalwart Tom Graveney might have altered Samuel's stance. Old school, but definitely not old fogey, he's quoted as saying: 'I will always defend a professional cricketer's right to maximise his earnings. There is no crime in that. Top cricketers are performers and entertainers of the highest order and just because we did it for peanuts in my time doesn't mean the modern generation should.

'Mine was the generation that would pack Lord's out for a five-day Test match and get paid a £75 match fee. We would be away on tour with the MCC to Australia and New Zealand for six months, filling huge arenas, and get paid a grand total of £550. Cricket was our life and passion, we didn't have to play of course, but frankly it was barely a living. Without your tax-free testimonial you had absolutely no chance of establishing yourself for a life after cricket.'

Now his 80s, it's just over 40 years since Tom dug in for an invaluable 76 against the Windies on the opening day of the First Test at Old Trafford and then found himself ingloriously chucked out of the England team - a cause célèbre that highlighted the financial plight of some very 'big' names. In many ways the reverberations are still being felt.

The year before Old Trafford Tom had arranged a testimonial game against a Bobby Simpson XI in Luton. It was scheduled for the Sunday – the rest day – of the Old Trafford Test. He had duly informed the England selectors, requesting that they omit him if the Luton game was a problem. It was time to put wife and family first. The guaranteed £1,000 from Luton was more than he would earn in an entire Test series.

England went ahead and picked him and he again told the selectors that he intended to honour his commitment in Luton. Tom duly drove down, smashed a few gentle full tosses from Richie Benaud to the boundary, and was back in Manchester for supper. The following day – his 42nd birthday – he was informed by public announcement while fielding that he was required at a MCC discipli-nary committee at Lord's on the Thursday. He was banned for three Tests. Enough was enough he decided, and retired from England duty.

On this train of thought, the name Ramnaresh Sarwan popped into my head, as did wretched 2005. As the spectre of dual relegations descended upon the Shire, Carl Greenidge, Tim Hancock, et al, were joined two-thirds the way through the season by the desperation signing. In a last ditch attempt stave off the unthink-able the Shire plumped for Sarwan. Originating from Wakenaam island at the mouth of the Guyana's Essequibo River, he was simply known as 'Ronnie'. He was a chap that took the Stanford dollar. Complete with diamond stud earrings, and later, in 2007, appointed captain of the West Indies, here was the very example of guy Samuel quibbled about.

In seven first-class matches for the Shire Ronnie scored 442 runs that included a century and one other fifty. Yet, Ronnie was thrown in at the deep end. August's return county match against Glamorgan saw the Shire slump to a humiliating 322 run defeat. Ronnie's presence in the batting order was of little effect. His contri-bution with bat being nought and a fifty, while his leg breaks failed to cripple any opposing batsman.

However, I kept stumm about the palavas from history allowing Samuel to remark that today few West Indians are involved in English county cricket. Of the eighteen counties, with a collective 450 cricketers on their respective annals, less than eighteen of them are West Indians - a poor statistic.

'What we need,' Samuel said, 'are more fellows like Courtney.'

'Courtney Walsh?'

'Yes, man. Do you remember him?'

'Cuddy? Absolutely! A weapon of regicide, and a Gloucestershire legend. Four-teen seasons with the Shire, a lovely bloke and a great sport.'

Samuel smiled. 'Mind you, his bowling was better than his use of the willow. Watch-ing him bat was poetry in action, but only if you had a delectation for Greek tragedy.'

How true, I thought, Cuddy still holds the unenviable record of scoring the most ducks in Test match cricket. What more could I add? Well, for over two decades he ran the equivalent of 1,000 miles in first-class cricket destroying metacarpals and careers with his bowling pace and guile. Now, the overseas pace bowler almost no longer exists in county cricket. He's too busy playing for his country, or in the Indian Premier League. A thought then occurred to me about a Nevisian noggin knocker. I smiled.

'So was Courtney as big a problem than your dentist?' I prompted Samuel.

Looking blank for a moment, recognition suddenly shone in Samuel's eyes. 'Oh, our DENTIST! Did you know Joey's back on the island? He's helping 'inspire' the school kids how to bowl.'

'Blimey, do the mums know?'

'Joey', better remembered as John 'The Dentist' Maynard had until recently been playing club cricket in the Yorkshire League. However, twenty years ago he had given Jack Russell and the rest of the England team a torrid time in two warm-up matches before their 1993/94 tour of the West Indies got even hotter. In the first he bruised out three of the England top order, Michael Atherton, Matthew Maynard and Nasser Hussain, and in the second, Graham Thorpe, Graeme Hick and Mark Ramprakash.

The tour itself left Peter Hayter of the *Mail on Sunday* reporting that England's 'ability to snatch defeat from the jaws of victory has left even the phlegmatic captain puzzled and bemused'. The locals of Nevis simply put it all down to confidence being dented by 'The Dentist'.

Born among the old plantations in Nevis' Gingerland district where Horatio Nelson lived and married and where Princess Diana's family still hold property, Joey is said to be the most famous Windies cricketer never to have played a test. He himself attributed the origins of the nickname to an incident when playing for Nevis against Antigua: 'There was this bloke playing for Antigua called Zorah Barthley, who was the West Indies youth team captain ... First thing in the morning he nicks one, but the umps didn't send him on his way. That wound me up a bit. And so the next ball was four yards quicker than anything I've ever bowled. He shaped to hook, and his teeth went flying all over the place. It was a funny old sight. But he was the man who made the Dentist really. I couldn't have done it without him.

'If you can't get them out, you gotta hurt them till they get out. I think I've pretty much broken every part of the body so far, from the teeth to the jaw, to the nose, to the ribs, to the arms and the toes. I never worry about hurting them at the time.'

Perish the thought what damage he might have done to the age-slowed reactions of Tim Hancock, et al, had Joey turned up in 2008. I could only reflect on the illuminating report of 1998 Ig Nobel Prize Winner Dr. Mara Sidoli of Washington, DC, *Farting as a Defence Against Unspeakable Dread*. Maybe that's what it was, I thought. Maybe, that's why there's no record of a last ball. Maybe, to a man, the MCC had run away from imagined catastrophe.

I shook the image away. 'What's Courtney doing now?' I said, bringing Samuel back from a far away look.

'Playing dominoes.' Samuel replied, having it on good authority that Courtney owns a sports bar and shop in Kingston where he lives. Here he regularly plays dominoes at the town's Melbourne Cricket Club. 'I travelled in the hope of watching him bowl once. But he didn't play.'

I asked Samuel where that had been. With the disappointment still seeming to show, he replied: 'Bristol. On their 1995 tour of England when the Windies beat Gloucestershire. I suppose Courtney didn't want to divide his loyalties.'

I commented that perhaps he was a bit excessive about not dividing them, he having once joked of never sealing the knot since his marriage to cricket was all consuming.

'I was that Bristol match, too. Filming,' I said. In that game Cuddy's partner in destruction Curtly Ambrose did happen to take the field. He had the ball speeding out of his hand at a rip-snorting 90mph plus from a height of 10 feet. But this was not before the silent assassin gave me a withering glare delivered with his pinch-eyed flintiness as I approached his personal space with my blessed TV camera. Further evidence of his mantra that 'Curtly talk to no man'.

Against England in the 1990s Curtly was awesome. Even Jack Russell, so often the boy stood on the burning deck as England collapsed around him, succumbed with the scorer writing 'b Ambrose' on an unlucky 13 instances. Now, both Cuddy and Curtly have been inducted into the ICC's Hall of Fame.

However, against the Shire Curtly was overshadowed, I recalled, by local unsung hero Kamran Sheeraz. It was a flash in the pan. Kamran got 'Man of the Match', yet he appears to have achieved diddly squat on the cricket field both before and after that Bristol occasion.

Obviously, the challenge posed by the Windies was Kamran's inspiration. And how. His medium-fast bowling laid waste to the tourists batting order, taking career best figures of 6 for 67 in the first innings. In the second he took 5 for 44. Combined, he achieved his only 10-wicket match haul in his first-class career. He memorably got Brian Lara out in both innings. Sadly, from a Shire point of view,

Tim Hancock and few of his teammates were a little 'noughty' in their batting.

Just before Samuel, hungry for his Sunday lunch, had eased into his aged car held together by God's will I remembered the ruddy scoresheet. I waved it in the air. 'Oh man, St. Kitts and Nevis won,' he called. 'Isn't it obvious. The last ball was a dot.'

How mundane. As Samuel drove away I gave thanks to a scorer for working on island time. That's to say, 'expeditiously'.

On my reluctant return to cold Blighty, I picked up on two bits of news. Firstly, Viagra aids jet lag recovery in hamsters, and secondly, Hamish Marshall had been selected for the MCC in the forthcoming county season curtain-raiser against champions Lancashire. The game was to be played under lights in Abu Dhabi using a pink ball. How wonderful. That would be a sight to see. Perhaps I could plan another holiday, I thought.

Report from the *Gloucestershire Gazette* 17th June 2005.

Match Celebrates Hancock's Heroics

The Tim Hancock Benefit match was held at Stone Cricket Club last week and was a huge success, with a strong Gloucestershire team gaining a 61-run victory over Stone.

The match, which took place at Stone's Swanley ground, was played in front of a whopping attendance of approximately 300 fans, with cricket lovers able to see some of the biggest names in the county.

Among them was fast bowler Jon Lewis, who starred for England on Monday in the country's first ever international Twenty20 match against Australia.

Lewis, who gained four wickets on Monday, actually opened the batting for Gloucestershire in the benefit match, scoring 72 as the visitors posted a total of 167-4.

Brad Thomas was the star of the Stone attack, claiming the wickets of Lewis and Hancock.

In reply, Stone finished on 106ao after a ruthless display of bowling from the county side. Once again, Thomas made a big impression as he hit 43, while Rockhampton guest star Will Tyler made 24. Sixteen-year-old Miles Palmer also caught the eye with his 18.

It was a memorable night for the club, with Hancock giving some coaching to a host of younger players before the game began. The match was a special tribute to the long-serving batsman, who has been at Gloucestershire since 1991.

SEVENTEEN

Sheepishness and Translation

'Who makes himself a sheep will be eaten by the wolves.'
Proverb.

The red ball game mattered to Goose, and myself. Even in early March.

Four years on, and we still chuntered about a piece by the journalist Frank Keating that appeared in the *Guardian* at the start of the 2008 cricket season. Frank hadn't minced his words: 'Sheepishly stirs another summer of what has tragically become a drawn-out primeval charade, the English County Championship. For decade upon decade it was a cherished adornment of the summer sub-culture, certainly for my generation when heroes were giants and giants were locals. About a quarter of a century ago the championship began fraying and then in no time unraveling. It is now a pointless exercise, unwatched, unwanted, serviced by mostly blinkered, greedy chairman-bullied committees and played by mostly unknown foreign and second-rate mercenaries.'

Oh dear, a few rings of truth maybe, but perhaps Frank hasn't spoken to anyone representative of the Shire. Here the Championship remains the Holy Grail, despite the shaky finances, poor attendances, and the irresistible rise of Twenty20 cricket.

But, it wasn't just Frank that had got our giddy goat.

'I blame HP. Him, and his ear trumpet,' said Goose, pointing his finger at a sauce bottle. 'It's all his fault. Thanks to the likes of him we're never goin' to win the Championship in my lifetime. Look at me. I'm a livin' wreck.' Goose downed the last swig of his cider pint. 'Another?' he said, heaving morosely to his feet. Gratefully, I handed over my empty glass.

Weaving away to bar, Goose left me to ruminate on porky scratchings.

HP was the nickname of Hubert Preston, a past editor of *Wisden Cricketers'
Almanack*. He was deaf for much of his life, using an ear trumpet before battery-
operated hearing aids became available. According to his notes in *Wisden's* 1949
edition, he was a strong supporter of the County Championship becoming two
divisions. In 2002, over half a century later, he posthumously got his way.

And now that the Shire was rooted in the second tier, neither Goose nor I could
see them get out of it. We weren't being unduly pessimistic. It was just that
Captain Giddo had gone on BBC Radio Gloucestershire earlier in the day, trying
to put on a brave face. Given the medium, the Shire's skipper was wasting his
time.

Giddo's sound bites were anything but cribbed from *Henry V*, or the speeches of
Sir Winston Churchill. Giddo had simply said it as it was. 'Things are beginning
to get that preseason feel about them … I'm pretty anxious to get outside netting
… just give it a whirl … it's a tough time for the club, we're aware of that … the
cavalry aren't coming … people are accustomed to how we're playing, so as a
group we'll find it harder to win so many games … the openers chewed up a
huge amount of balls.'

Oh my, oh my.

Cash flow problems in cricket have a positive habit of giving youth a chance. This
had done the trick in the past.

Take the puny looking Charlie Townsend, a leg break bowler from Clifton
College. At the age of 16 in 1893 he took 21 first-class wickets in four games and
showed, despite his build, the ability to get a lot of overs under his belt, and spin
the ball prodigiously from leg. In that season, Shire wicky, William Brain,
completed the only instance of a first-class hat-trick of stumpings - all taken off
Charlie's bowling.

And come August 1895, the lad became a phenomenon during his summer holidays. Schoolwork meant he'd only played one match up to the last week of July,
achieving just a couple of expensive wickets. However, free as a lark, he bagged
122 victims in the Shire's remaining eleven matches. And to top things off, he
scored a couple of centuries, as well.

Today, there is a desperate need for youth to pull its weight, even more than J.M.
Barrie, the creator of *Peter Pan*, could have imagined in the 1920s when he
designed and had built the cute thatched larch wood walled pavilion that's stood
on staddle stone mushrooms at Stanway.

Rumours abounded that old stagers like former Shire skip Chris Taylor were saying adieu. Those of catholic taste prayed to the saints for salvation.

Therefore, to make known St. George boasted a cricket club could swell an Englishman's heart with hope, until it's revealed the St George in question has nowt to do with a dragon, and much more to do with the *Worlds End*, the pub on Clouds Hill Road, offering regular karaoke. Here Goose and I eavesdropped as wags joked about the 'Four from St George' whom, according to a certain international cricketer plying his trade at the Shire, were on 'a pretty even scope' when it came to brightness. And he made no mention of halos. Nor did he intimate that, with money being in short supply, there was a fear of the Gladiators changing into Gladirags.

Yet, as if to lampoon the Four Riders of the Apocalypse, Shire whippersnappers Chris Dent, Jack Taylor, James Fuller and David Payne, I was told, had emerged from the end of the line – the tramline. Knowledgeable Bristolians will ask whether the 'Four' know their coal from their fireclay before informing those interested that St George was the pits. They're not being rude. Once a mining area, now only pit names and a tall thin chimney topping Troopers Hill remain as reminders of the past.

As with mining communities anywhere, be they from Yorks, Notts, Zum, or the Shire, tough fine cricketers surfaced. But with the mines gone, the jury's still out on the connected four.

Until about 1860, St. George enjoyed its Gloucestershire independence outside the Bristol boundary. The tramline, though, allowed the bowels of the mines to connect to the city's heart. And there, where the line had begun, is a place to discover reactionaries of sorts.

The reason for this, perhaps a tad facetiously, can be found in precedent.

When Northants made 12 all out and 40 for 7 in June 1907, it doesn't seem right thinking of Edward Dennett, his thumb and forefinger having pointed the waxed ends of his immaculate handle bar moustache, spinning out 15 wickets for 24 runs at the Spa Ground, Gleawecestre. Read the word. G-L-E-A-W-E-C-E-S-T-R-E. It's a tongue-twister. Try spelling it, eyes closed.

Thankfully, long before the age of first class cricket 'Gloucester' tripped off the tongue, and the town rewarded itself with a mint. That's to say the town made dosh rather than sharing some humbug.

Now, the Euro is in trouble, the world's financial system is in turmoil. A perfect time say Bristolians to make *their* own money. Hail the 'Bristol Pound'. Backed by the city council it will be printable, and online and mobile phone tradable.

Wonderful. But could the local wonga bail the Shire out of its predicament? Could Gladirags become a word of the past. Experts are non-committal on both counts.

Well, that's the rumour emanating from council offices within the old St Nicholas' Church, a former place of worship still holding a Hogarth altarpiece triptych as collateral, as well as a forgotten cricket tie.

Although, in not wanting to confuse the issue, whether the Reverend William Goldwin had a cricket tie or not, there isn't the foggiest notion. To be fair, William is a bit of an enigma. He attended Eton and then graduated to King's College, Cambridge in 1700 before subsequently becoming a Master of Bristol Grammar School, and, until his death in 1747, Vicar of St Nicholas'.

Other certainties about William are his having an educated skill in Latin, and a true love of the game. Put the two together, and one gets something today that's as accessible as Malayalam. For example:

> Ver venit, cum mitis et liquidi caeli
> Subridens, cum misericordiam coaxes terra ferre
> Et activa pedes ad quot ubi agros late;
> A bigas iuvenes crocken vespertiliones suppleverunt.

These are just four of ninety-five graceful lines that as a whole constituted cricket's earliest known work of literature. From him the likes of John Arlott and Henry Blofeld did follow.

William's subject was a rural cricket match. Called *In Certamen Pilae* (*On a Ball Game*), it was published in his set of poems *Musae Juveniles* in March 1706. It was only thanks to Harry Perry and P.F. Thomas that we can read William's lines in English.

> Springtime comes, with mild and limpid air
> Smiling, with kindness coaxes earth to bear
> And active feet to sport where fields spread wide;
> A team of youths with crocken bats supplied.

Basically, the story goes as follows. In early spring a chosen 'cohort' of youths, armed with curved bats, 'descends rejoicing to the field'. Each team does its best to impose its own laws, until a grey-haired chap 'composes' the squabble. The pitch is marked out and a single bail is placed on the stumps that 'cry out for good defence' against 'the leathern sphere'. Two umpires stand 'leaning on their bats' while the scorers 'sit on a hummock ready to cut the mounting score on sticks with their little knives'.

After the game begins, a batsman 'propels the strident ball afar,' but a clear-sighted fielder prepares his 'ambush in the deep, and with outstretched palms joyfully accepts it as it falls'. Grief overwhelms those who silently mourn their mate's disaster.

Similar to recent Shire woes, a tale of misfortune continues. One batter, in going for a second run, 'falls headlong at the very foot of the wicket' making the 'shaken earth groans beneath his great weight,' as the rustic throng piddle themselves with laughter.

The other side fares better, and 'Victory, long striven for, noisily flaps its wings and fills the sky with the shouts and roars of success'.

Back in the *Worlds End,* several bar crooners having failed to delight with renditions of *'I did it my way',* much head scratching arrived at William's reason for using highfaluting Latin. It was simple. He was trying to limit attention, and so preserve his dog-collared social reputation. This was because, from the perspective of an indignant John Stow writing a few years before William, 'only the common sort diverted themselves at cricket, wrestling, cudgels, ninepins, shovelboard, football, ringing of bells, quoits, pitching the ball, bull and bear baiting, throwing cocks, and lying in the alehouses'. It was far too early to mention rugby and dwarf throwing.

Oh, how times have changed. Men and women in *Worlds End* happily admitted their guilt on charges one and twelve. Pint in hand, they vehemently denied, in any way, of being common sorts.

But, it wasn't just William who was penning away in Latin. Others did, too. Though they preferred to remain anonymous, like the clever scribbler of *Clava Falcata Torsio (Playing Ball with a Curved Bat).* Dating from 1723 it appeared as a translation in *The Cricket Statistician,* no. 148, Winter 2009.

Describing a one innings affair, 'true friends divide into two lines'. This probably meant the old school habit of teams being alternately picked by self-appointed captains on a basis of 'I'll have … Frederick,' … 'Oh well, in that case I'll have … Montague,' before ending up with the last remaining team choices - the awkward weakest links.

In addition, there is allusion to something quite contemporary, an idea that seems to have stuck, and is used today in Test matches – having a quartet of officialdom. In 1723, a game's control was in the hands of 'four men of whom two safeguard the laws of one wicket and two the other'.

Nearly three hundred years later other things also remain unchanged. Attention is drawn to 'goading, tantrums, triumphs and celebrations' not to mention cricket's darker side. The litigious 'No-Ballgate', perhaps, is still fresh in the mind. However, it's cause is not a unique problem. *Clava Falcata Torsio* reports substantial match betting. Indeed, put in today's money, a single bet equivalent to one-and-a-quarter million quid was placed on the outcome of a match. One can only surmise how long that would take to print in Bristol pounds.

Given even a small percentage of such a fortune the Shire could obtain the services of experienced international cricketing talent to bolster confidence.

Failing that, it's probably down to the 'Four from St George'. And, of course, there is precedent for even bowlers raised on the field of St George to have the habit of batting most capably. Jack Bessant was one. Picked up by the Shire in 1923, he was a bowler capable of running through any side. Yet, he and Robert Gouldsworthy still hold their county's 10th wicket partnership record after sharing a stand of 131 against Somerset at Bristol in 1923.

Goose plonked a cider in front of my schnozzle. 'That'll put the world to rights,' he said.

'Bless you,' I responded, reaching for the cloudy elixir. 'We'll just have to wait and see.' After all, Giddo had ended on the positive note of, 'perhaps we can surprise a few people.'

As Goose went to partake of the karaoke, it crossed my mind whether Giddo's 'outside netting' was for the raspberries.

GLOUCESTERSHIRE v NORTHAMPTONSHIRE
County Championship 1907

Spa Ground, Gloucester on 10th, 11th, 12th June 1907 (3-day match)
Gloucestershire won the toss and decided to bat
Umpires: A Millward, JE West
Close of play day 1: Gloucestershire (1) 20/4 (Jessop 4*)
Close of play day 2: Northamptonshire (2) 40/7 (Thompson 5*, King 1*)
No play day 3 – rain.

Gloucestershire first innings

EP Barnett	lbw	b Thompson	3
H Wrathall		b Thompson	4
+JH Board		b Thompson	3
MG Salter	c Buswell	b East	3
*GL Jessop		b East	22
RTH Mackenzie		b East	0
T Langdon		b East	4
HJ Huggins	c Crosse	b East	8
EJ Spry	lbw	b Thompson	6

CWL Parker	not out		2
EG Dennett	c Pool	b Thompson	0
Extras (2 b, 3 lb)			5
Total (all out, 32.5 overs)			60

Fall of wickets:
1-4, 2-13, 3-14, 4-20, 5-20, 6-32, 7-45, 8-58, 9-60, 10-60 (32.5 ov)

Northamptonshire bowling	Overs	Mdns	Runs	Wkts
Thompson	16.5	7	29	5
East	16	5	26	5

Northamptonshire first innings

*EM Crosse	c Board	b Dennett	4
M Cox	lbw	b Dennett	2
CJT Pool	c Spry	b Dennett	4
+WA Buswell	st Board	b Dennett	1
LT Driffield		b Dennett	0
GJ Thompson		b Dennett	0
RWR Hawtin	lbw	b Dennett	0
W East	st Board	b Dennett	0
RN Beasley		b Jessop	1
S King	not out		0
W Wells	c Parker	b Jessop	0
Extras			
Total (all out, 11.3 overs)			12

Fall of wickets:
1-6, 2-10, 3-11, 4-11, 5-11, 6-11, 7-11, 8-12, 9-12, 10-12 (11.3 ov)

Gloucestershire bowling	Overs	Mdns	Runs	Wkts
Dennett	6	1	9	8
Jessop	5.3	4	3	2

Gloucestershire second innings

RTH Mackenzie	c King	b East	21
T Langdon	lbw	b Thompson	4
H Wrathall		b Thompson	7
+JH Board	lbw	b Thompson	5
*GL Jessop	c Hawtin	b East	24
MG Salter	c and b East		3
EP Barnett		b East	0
HJ Huggins	c Buswell	b East	3
EJ Spry		b East	4
CWL Parker	not out		8

EG Dennett	b East	0

Extras (9 b)		9
Total (all out, 29.2 overs)		88

Fall of wickets:
1-17, 2-35, 3-35, 4-52, 5-57, 6-57, 7-68, 8-77, 9-88, 10-88 (29.2 ov)

Northamptonshire bowling	Overs	Mdns	Run	Wkts
Thompson	15	2	43	3
East	14.2	4	36	7

Northamptonshire second innings

*EM Crosse	c and b Dennett		0
M Cox	c Barnett	b Dennett	12
RWR Hawtin	lbw	b Dennett	8
CJT Pool	st Board	b Dennett	9
GJ Thompson	not out		5
RN Beasley		b Dennett	0
+WA Buswell	c Langdon	b Dennett	0
W East	lbw	b Dennett	2
S King	not out		1
LT Driffield	did not bat		
W Wells	did not bat		
Extras (2 b, 1 lb)			3
Total (7 wickets, 30 overs)			40

Fall of wickets:
1-4, 2-17, 3-26, 4-31, 5-31, 6-31, 7-33

Gloucestershire bowling	Overs	Mdns	Runs	Wkts
Dennett	15	8	12	7
Jessop	10	3	20	0
Parker	5	2	5	0

Match drawn

A Bat Maker's Story

When the spring sun shines, mention 'Hunts' in Gloucester and it's likely neither the Beaufort nor the Vale of the White Horse is on your mind. Instead, you're probably cogitating about cricket bats.

The old Moreland Match Factory may have closed in 1976, but to say anything made there today amidst the lathes, mallets, grinders, chisels and sawdust is no better than 'matchwood' would be downright insulting. Yet, not wishing to sound finickity, to the naïve a cricket bat is just that.

Martin Berrill promises to put such ideas well and truly straight by making some of the finest examples of cricket bat in the country. To his mind there's willow and there's … well, willow. Although, when I caught up with him at an inopportune moment he must have wished he were less of a bat maker and more of an octopus.

He was trawling through the inboxes of two computers trying to find an email whilst having to tackle three simultaneous phone conversations. One sounded like blue murder. 'Stick it in the chest!' he ordered. And his words into another mouthpiece were anything other than reassuring. 'No, not you, Tracy. I'll get back to you as soon as I'm free. Probably in six months.' And into the third, 'I can't see any evidence. When did you say you sent it? …. Can I get back to you? I've a shop full of people baying for me.'

The last point I quite understood. It was a Friday morning and, with the weather set fair, Martin had customers to satisfy. In this he's often likened to Mr Ollivander, the Diagon Alley wand maker in *Harry Potter*. Bat choosing is a process of elimination. Martin remembers every bat he's ever sold. Every single one. Trial bats in the shop often pile up like Jenga as the perfect match between bat and bod is sought.

'All my bats are guaranteed to make a century every innings,' he told me before chuckling, ' I can't guarantee the individual holding it.' Never was a truer word spoken in jest. With one of Martin's bats in their hands, Courtney Walsh and New Zealand's Danny Morrison vied with one another for the most number of international ducks. It's something that still makes Martin wince.

Happily, he's proud to say Charlotte Edwards, the captain of England Women's cricket, is currently one of his more adept clients. Other names tripped off his tongue as if reciting an academy of fame – Rod Marsh, Imran Khan and David Gower. After uttering 'Monty Panesar' Martin gave a sudden nervous cough. This I learned was nothing to do with Monty's batting prowess. Rather it was a demand to Martin to pay him 'a large sum of money' for the privilege of using a Hunts bat. I remarked I'd check on Monty's current blade at the earliest opportunity.

As for himself, Martin, now in his very early 50s had retired his own cricket gear into a squinch for spiders somewhere at the back of his garage. However, it doesn't seem too long ago since he was playing in the Stroud League for King's Stanley whose Marling Close ground was once fraternized by film stars. Here Roy Bassett stumped both Kenneth Moore and Basil Rathbone. And here Martin scored centuries with a bat that he'd lovingly crafted himself after moving to Gloucester in 1986. By then he had nine years of bat making experience behind him.

His first year in the trade had been marvellous. He'd delighted in both Geoffrey Boycott and John Edrich scoring their respective hundredth hundred wielding the Hunts County bats he'd helped to make while working in St Neots beside the Great Ouse river in Cambridgeshire. They were idyllic days.

Back then Hunts grew their own willow trees. Drawn into nostalgia Martin was proud to have made a bat from one and used it to score a century. Until the custom died with the '70s the company's willows were actually grown on an island in the middle of the Great Ouse and, when chopped, the logs had to be floated downriver to the point of collection.

'Didn't that make the bats a bit damp,' I asked, thinking of the corkscrew hazel in a dark dank corner of my garden and ahead of Martin explaining that Hunts religiously dried their timber in stacks slowly over a period of time, swopping top for bottom three or four times a year. It was this process that taught him to grade a chunk of willow.

Also, one can accurately say he can 'read' a cricket bat. The difference between English and Kashmir willow disgusts him. The latter wood is whiter and the grain prouder, and not in a good sense. For to make a blade smooth requires the job of grinding, not gentle sanding. Those wanting to know about performance, it's the difference between 'ping' and 'clunk'.

My confiding to having bought a *Hero Honda* for a quid off the internet only to feed the bloody thing to an autumn bonfire after a single innings

of two balls ended by middling a gentle full toss limply to mid-on rather proved Martin's point.

And he bemoans the influx of other cheap subcontinent cricket merchandise, too. Under his desk is a box of about thirty half balls that he's sawn in two. 'The rubbish they put inside has to be seen to be believed,' he said getting his gander up. 'There's scrunched up silver paper and everything. The balls don't just go out of shape, they go biscuit flat.'

To Martin, the makeup of a cricket ball touches a nerve in him. Between 1981 and 1985 he was hand stitching them in Australia. Four years of bruised and needle impaled fingers was enough for him. Although he vehemently disagreed with me that it must have been 'convict work', he thought it much better sticking to making bats.

And in our changing times he has achieved this with aplomb in Gloucester. Despite being forced to source his English willow from the Essex wholesalers AS Wright he reckons he's one in a small minority of only ten or fifteen master craftsman bat makers remaining in England. He can't get apprentices to carry on tradition for love nor money. Young people want to work with computers instead of with their hands, he maintains. So long may Martin continue to be the stoic.

With his staff becoming increasingly agitated I left this octopus man of declining breed to his admiring customers and his Jenga, hoping at the same time he'd avoid committing blue murder. Mr Ollivander, indeed.

Now, what if he could just grow himself a Whomping Willow, I thought. That would make cricketing weekends around Gloucester and beyond sublime.

If Gloucestershire Were A Celebrity

'If Gloucestershire were a celebrity it would be Silvio Berlusconi. A charming old stager who seems to have been around for ages, but could be in trouble quite soon if their gamble of investing heavily in youth backfires.'

Graham Clutton, *The Telegraph Review,* 2011.

EIGHTEEN

Celandines and Snow

'What do they know of cricket, who only cricket know?'
C.L.R. James (Afro-Trinidadian cricket writer, 1901-1989).

And so began Captain Giddo's benefit season. Lambs gamboled. Their counterparts, the youthful players of the Shire, blinked sleepily, awaking to Captain's brother Will being media hailed as 'the one to watch'. He'd certainly silenced the pessimists following his arrival from Durham. A first Gloucestershire season of first-class cricket was marked by passing those two key landmarks for an all-rounder: scoring over 1,000 runs and taking more than 50 Championship wickets. Far from being outshone by his older sibling, Will had topped the county's batting averages at 45.72 and was also the most economical of the Shire's regular main line bowlers.

His services would be an essential. Chris Taylor had joined in the unsettling fad of migration. The County had been quick to scotch the rumours that he was joining Zum until he'd actually pitched up in Taunton with his 'specialist field-ing' coach's bag as hedge bank celandines and primroses bloomed yellow in the Spring sunshine.

And I wracked my brains of a way to break it to Goose gently that Kevin O'Brien was also rocking off in Taylor's direction.

On the up side, Mr Balmer now offered Surrey Cricket Loam delivered to the club door at 'competitive' prices, as well as discounted supplies of 'cricket grass seed, fertilisers and chemicals'.

Suddenly, the Shire was abuzz with news. It was the year of the London

Olympics. German TV, bless it, had done a spin on Weltanshauung, that's to say, how one sees the world: 'it'll rain. There'll be riots. The food's crap. The stadiums are hideous.'

Some wags suggested the comments were more appropriate if aimed at the Shire.

In Brockworth people had been spat at in the street, received verbal abuse in shops and at school gates. There had even been talk of bricks through windows and houses being burned down. Why? Because the decision had been taken to kill off the official Cheese Rolling Festival on Cooper's Hill.

But this was merely a distraction to the unexpected growth of 'Bristle's' Lib Dems becoming highly unpopular. The City Council had moved by six votes to four to turn down plans to redevelop the County Ground. On Twitter Captain Giddo, exclaimed it was 'unbelievable' and that WG Grace would have been 'gutted'.

A spokesman for the Howzat Residents' Group was cock-a-hoop, while Club executive Tom Richardson was 'considering' whether the bombshell meant the end of first class cricket at Nevil Road. Moving to the Tuffley Wagon Works was a no-no because of being wanted by Gordon League Rugby Football Club. And a runway at Filton Airport, also a possibility, attracted the headline: 'Cricket club's future uncertain'.

But in the meantime it was business as usual when the calendar finally turned to April.

Across the South West clubs like Roadwater CC suggested thermals and galoshes be worn for the first outdoor nets.

At Nevil Road, as the Shire busied itself with interviews, photos and meeting sponsors at the preseason launch, it became clear some part of last season's meagre profit had already been spent. 'Just been in the Gloscricket dressing room bit of a mess!' tweeted James Ayland, 'Must be all the new kit!'

Beside the M5 the clever rooks at Michael Wood Services began to gather their expertise at the bins, awaiting the pit-stop rubbish of optimistic supporters making their way to Chelmsford for the season's opening game. The flickering memory of the Shire's biggest ever innings victory in their history had happened in Essex. Okay, that was in 1998, but what the hell, last season the Shire had drawn with the 'Eaglemen' twice in the eerie silence of the Championship.

'Caution, caution,' a little voice said, Kane Williamson wasn't due for another week or so.

And, oh dear. Yes, the odd one kept low and the odd one fizzed – but it wasn't a bad wicket. Essex had shown the way with 364 all out in their first innings without drowning in honey, I mean, buffet bowling, the type of which some batters indulge once too often.

Come day 2 and the Shire lost 15 wickets before bad light brought a merciful close, despite host skipper Foster's earnest chin-wag with the umpires. Only Chris Dent and Dan Housego offered resistance in a first innings procession that wobbled to 180. Second time around, much to Essex glee, the wobble was worse. A hash, really - the Shire top order blown away by Masters and Napier. Captain Giddo castled for 0. Hamish Marshall ell bee for not a lot, and Ian Cockbain twisted an ankle.

After about an hour on the morning of day 3 it was all over. But at least the Shire went down all guns blazing. Will Gidman did his best, but his ell bee to a jaffer triggered a wickets rush. Ed Young and Ian Saxelby then made the last stand a stoic one. When the inevitable came the deficit on Essex's first innings had been reduced to a tolerable 38, and it was time to go home. The music of BBC Radio Bristol awaited. Captain Giddo prepared a cautious statement.

'It was a pretty harsh lesson,' he said on air, 'hopefully in a few weeks we'll look back on it and realise it was a good thing.' Bless him, true to his word within a day or two he had the Shire dusted down and smartened up and ready to travel to Southampton.

I asked myself whether there were others like me who couldn't get it into their noggin that the Rose Bowl was now the Aegus Bowl, preventing witticisms about Hampshire hogs being delicate petals.

In addition, I almost felt it necessary to enquire whether the Shire, batting first this time, still suffered the Chelmsford trembles. But with the high tech scoreboard on 22 for 2, Chris Dent seemed calm and collected at the crease. Masterfully, he went on to become the Shire's primary centurion of the campaign. By day 4, in what was something of turn up for the book, Hampshire, needing 290 to win, were in a right 'Royal' mess between rain showers.

And with the home side wading to 72 for 6, things were going swimmingly for Captain Giddo and his men. Then the trembles returned as the hogs stirred their loins and began to battle.

'Glos making a horlicks of it at the Rose Bowl. 210-7 now. Nightmare.' tweeted the ether. 'Oh heck!' came a reply. There is another calling it the Rose Bowl, thought I.

Two boils of the kettle hailed the arrival of a positive phone tapping. 'Hants 247 - 9. Tight finish!'

Elsewhere Langley CC's pitch preparation turned into sheep herding.

I diverted myself from nervous West Country desk drumming to tweet to Lowerhouse CC 'I'm right behind you – from afar' as they cruised to victory amongst falling snowflakes and bruising hailstones into Round 2 of the Lancashire Cup.

And whereas my Uncle Tubby had Gloucestershire blood in his veins, by extending the friendship of the 'cricket family' Langwith CC, somewhere in the East Midland borderlands of Notts and Derbys, completely discombobulated me. This was where my Mum and Gran had had their soul and roots. I felt another sudden emotional tug. Cricket family loyalties can be so very fickle, but for the moment it was best to focus on the Shire.

Finally an end was put to the Saints' saga. 'Hants all out 256. Last gasp win for Glos by 33 runs!' Thrilling stuff, indeed. And Will, the golden boy of the moment, on emerging with 9 for 114, added to Chris Dent's match contribution, had placed the Shire third in the Championship table.

Beside his cup of tea profile picture, Captain Giddo tweeted: 'Thanks for all the messages today. Great win against a good team. Hard work but really enjoyable.'

Living in the moment, optimism for the future had suddenly become bouncy. Almost a full County season lay ahead in what can best be described as a 'State of Grace'.

I'd found the spirit of Gloucestershire cricket was wonderfully alive and well not just upon Sheepscombe's Laurie Lee Field. With the old wizard Murali back in Gladiator blue for the slog fests joined by the raw young talent of Graeme McCarter emerging from the wings, as Goose would say, 'Bring it on'.

> *'The old order changeth, yielding place to new.'*
> Lord Alfred Tennyson

Rain Stopped Play

NINETEEN

A Bit of Head Scratching

'The heart that truly loves never forgets.'
Proverb.

1. Name the Gloucestershire player who remains the only player ever to hit a ball from the Adelaide Oval into the Torrens River.

2. What year did the Gloucester Diocesan Clergy Cricket Club win the *Church Times* Cricket Cup?

3. What links Sherlock Holmes and photographs of fairies with W.G. Grace?

4. Name the post-war Gloucestershire bowler with the same letters in both his Christian and surnames.

5. Name the Durham batsman who carried his bat for 158 against Gloucestershire at Gateshead Fell in 1994.

6. Name the Gloucestershire bowler with match figures of 14 for 169 at Taunton in 1993.

7. G.A. Beet was the appropriately named twelfth man who caught four catches in an innings against his own team as a substitute fielder for Gloucestershire in 1959. Name his team.

8. Name the New Zealand tourist in 1927 who in a quarter of an hour scored 50 against Gloucestershire and was then invited to join the county.

9. How in 1973 did W.G. Grace get to become in company with the Queen?

10. Name the Gloucestershire cricketer of shuffling feet and many centuries who after only one game for England was promptly dropped because of his atrocious fielding.

11. Born in 1893 at Cheltenham and nicknamed 'Bernie', name the left-handed batsman and slow left-armer who played for Gloucestershire between 1919 and 1932.

12. Name the cricket ground in Stroud last played on in 1970 that became buried under part of the Bath Road Trading Estate.

13. Name the pacey seam bowling Lance Corporal of the Royal Signals Corps who swapped barracks for bouncers by signing a Gloucestershire contract in 2010.

14. Name the well-known commentator who took the microphone for Lashings first match of the 2011 season when, led by Phil DeFreitas, they played Rockhampton.

15. Born in Hammersmith, who played for Gloucestershire between 1991 and 1993 before ending his playing career at Worcestershire and going on to become a television presenter for France 24 and Russia Today?

16. Name the Gloucetershire captain, who in 1936 died from car crash injuries suffered near Cirencester when driving home from the last game of the season.

17. Andrew Symonds hit a world record number of sixes at Abergavenny while playing for Gloucestershire. He also played for Australia. Where was he born?

18. Name the school in Gloucester where the Gladiators staged T20 matches in 2010 and 2011.

19. Name the chap who batted 602 times for Gloucestershire, averaged a paltry 5.43 including 18 pairs, and once had five successive ducks.

20. Despite winning fifteen of their games in 1930 Gloucestershire finished runners-up in the County Championship to a county that had won only ten. Which county was it?

21. In 1962 Gloucestershire made their first overseas tour. Name the captain.

22. Name the Gloucestershire all rounder born in Georgetown in 1958.

23. Name the Gloucestershire batsman who scored a century before lunch against both Glamorgan and Somerset in 1934 and was in the 1938 England side along with Wally Hammond and Tom Goddard in the infamous Third Test at Old Trafford against Australia in which, to the delight of the cartoonists of the day, not a ball was bowled in the five days.

24. There are 13 First Class pitches on the Ground at Nevil Road. In 2008 the idea arose for supporters to have their name dedicated to one of those pitches for a ten year period in return for a nominated donation towards the cost of what?

25. In 1929 Gloucestershire won at the Gloucester Wagon works. With less than an hour and a half left to play on the final day, name the Gloucestershire captain who declared the county's first innings one run ahead of Middlesex with the words: 'Got to let the dog see the rabbit.'

Answers in Appendix One

APPENDIX ONE

Answers to a Bit of Head Scratching

1. Gilbert Jessop. In 1966 a Gilbert Jessop Society was founded in Australia. A Jessop collection is now housed in the Adelaide University Law Library.

2. 1973.

3. Sir Arthur Conan Doyle. The famous writer who claimed a set of photographs proved the existence of fairies, also claimed just one first-class wicket. It was the Big 'Un's.

4. Brian Brain.

5. Wayne Larkins.

6. Martyn Ball.

7. Derbyshire.

8. C.C. Dacre.

9. He appeared on a set of three cricket stamps to commemorate one hundred years of county cricket.

10. Alf Dipper. In 1932 he left Gloucestershire to become a first-class umpire.

11. Bernard Bloodworth.

12. The Erinoid Ground.

13. David Wade.

14. Henry 'Blowers' Blofeld.

15. Jason de la Peña.

16. Dallas Page.

17. Birmingham.

18. King's.

19. Sam Cook.

20. Lancashire.

21. Tom Pugh.

22. Monty Lynch.

23. Charlie Barnett.

24. A new scoreboard. In 2009 a framed chart containing the names of all the 'Pitch Supporters' was unveiled in the Grace Room. The chart will remain in the Grace room until it's placed in the club museum.

25. Bev Lyon.

Gloucestershire Records for those with the desire to know

First-Class Cricket

Highest total:	For 695-9d v. Middlesex	Gloucester	2004
	V. 774-7d by Australians	Bristol	1948
Lowest total:	For 17 v. Australians	Cheltenham	1896
	V. 12 by Northants	Gloucester	1907
Highest innings:	For 341 CM Spearman v. Middlesex	Gloucester	2004
	V. 319 CJL Rogers for Northants	Northampton	2006
Best Bowling:	For 10-40 EG Dennett v. Essex	Bristol	1906
(innings	V. 10-66 AA Mailey for Australians	Cheltenham	1921
	10-66 K Smales for Notts	Stroud	1956
Best Bowling	For 17-56 CWL Parker v. Essex	Gloucester	1925
(match)	V. 15-87 AJ Conway for Worcs	Morton-in-M	1914

Most Runs – Season	2860	WR Hammond (av 69.75)		1933
Most Runs - Career	33664	WR Hammond (av 57.05)		1920 – 51
Most 100s - Season	13	WR Hammond		1938
Most 100s - Career	113	WR Hammond		1920 - 51
Most wkts - Season	222	TWJ Goddard (av 16.80)		1937
	222	TWJ Goddard (av 16.37)		1947
Most wkts - Career	3170	CWL Parker (av 19.43)		1903 - 35
Most Career W-K Dismissals	1054	RC Russell 950ct 104st		1981-2004
Most Career Catches in field	719	CA Milton		1948 -74

Limited-Overs Cricket

Highest total:	50ov	401-7 v. Bucks	Wing	2003
	40ov	366-6 v. Northants	Cheltenham	2001
	T20	244-3 v. Middlesex	Uxbridge	2011
Lowest total:	50ov	82 v. Notts	Bristol	1987
	40ov	49 v. Middlesex	Bristol	1978
	T20	68 v. Hampshire	Bristol	2010
Highest innings:	50ov	177 AJ Wright v. Scotland	Bristol	1997
	40ov	153 CM Spearman v. Warks	Gloucester	2003
	T20	119 KJ O'Brien v. Middlesex	Uxbridge	2011
Best Bowling :	50ov	6-21 CA Walsh v. Kent	Bristol	1990
		6-21 CA Walsh v. Cheshire	Bristol	1992
	40ov	7-29 DA Payne v. Essex	Chelmsford	2010
	T20	4-16 JMR Taylor v. Somerset	Bristol	201

E N D P I E C E

'As sure as God is in Gloucester.'
                    Proverb.

I'm confident the pantheon of Gloucestershire greats is preserved in the cricket fields of Elysium. Somewhere among the daisies my Uncle Tubby will be bowling through his cat-flap, his batting technique no doubt frowned at by those recent arrivals Arthur Milton, Bert Avery, 'Bomber' Wells, and Peter West. Close by, David Shepherd will surely be chuckling and hopping merrily.